# ADVENTURES

# IN

# DISCIPLESHIP

## ON GOD'S TEAM

### MICHAEL PEARSON

Cover Design: 99Designs.com

Cover Image: Shutterstock.com / 547233985

ISBN: 978-1-7360482-0-7

# DEDICATION

To my son, Michael Trevon Pearson. From the day you were born, my prayer for you has been that you would have a heart that pursues God. I am so grateful to have such an amazing son. I love you so much!

To my mother, Elizabeth Jean (Betty Jean or BJ) Pearson. You were an anchor and guiding light in my life. You were a constant source of unconditional love and an excellent example of how to live a humble and righteous life. I look forward to the day when I can be where you are now: basking in the glorious presence of Jesus!

# ACKNOWLEDGMENTS

I would like to thank Jami-Jon Mitchell Pearson, who originally compiled much of this material from my earlier writings under the title, The Maturing Heart.

I would also like to thank my brother, David Pearson, and my friends, Garron Gianopulos and Eddie Isom for editing help and feedback.

Most importantly, I would like to thank my Father in heaven for fathering me through so many of my deceptions, distractions, and shortcomings. I would like to thank my Savior, Jesus, for His patient and steadfast love. And finally, I would like to thank my Power Source, the Holy Spirit, who makes everything come together for His good.

# CONTENTS

# MORE THAN AN INTRODUCTION

Our journey with God starts in a single moment - with a conviction, a decision, and a surrender. But this new, spiritual birth is just the beginning. At its core, Christianity is a relationship with the Christ. And like any relationship, our relationship with Jesus was always designed to grow and mature over time.

Unfortunately, as life goes on, many people begin to lose their love and passion for God. They become spiritually comfortable and quit pursuing Him with all their heart. As a result, they become apathetic to the things that God is most passionate about.

Within the first couple of years after a person puts their faith in Jesus Christ, they are often excited and seem likely to tell others about Him. Some knock on doors, hand out tracts, or go on short missions trips. But if they do not experience significant results, they get discouraged and their passion to introduce other people to Jesus drops to almost nothing and often remains there for the rest of their lives.

i

How sad! This must grieve the heart of God.

Sure, the excitement and freedom is a big motivation in the beginning, but this long-term love-loss is not part of God's plan. He designed us to grow closer and more intimate with Him as we experience life's ups and downs and challenges together. God designed all relationships to reflect our relationship with Him. Our closeness with our spouse, kids, and friends is also designed to grow deeper as we laugh, struggle, offend and forgive each other. Our trust in God should grow as we see His faithfulness through a variety of situations. As we spend time in God's presence, our love for Him grows as we see Him more clearly and understand His character more fully.

The Bible says we are to consider one another in order to stir up love and good works (Hebrews 10:24). But we cannot love or do good works if we do not see things from God's perspective. We must not allow ourselves to become Biblically illiterate. How can we worship God in spirit and in truth if we do not know what is true? The Bible is as relevant for us today as it was for the people it was originally written for. The Bible clearly shows us how to walk with God in a way that pleases and glorifies Him.

In this book, we will focus on a few Bible verses that are either so familiar that they may have lost their meaning or verses that are often overlooked altogether. We will then apply these passages to our lives today in order to draw us closer to God.

Our salvation is assured and we are given eternal life the moment we place our faith in Jesus Christ and let the blood He shed on the cross wash away our sins. This book addresses the "Now what?" that hits us after that life-changing spiritual re-birth takes place. This book is about walking with Jesus and abiding in Him. It is about hearing His Word, taking it to heart, and then taking up our cross every day in order to follow Him.

***This is where the first part of our great adventure begins!***

Over the next 40 days, try to get into the habit of making the Word of God personal. We should not just want to read the Bible, we should strive to live the Bible. But to do that our motive cannot be to read the Bible just to know it, we must read it to know Him. Ultimately, we should adore the Author, the Word that was made flesh and dwelt among us.

At the end of each lesson, there are a few other Bible verses listed that will help you dig a little deeper into the topic that was discussed. You are strongly encouraged to take a few extra minutes to read through them. The more passages we read on a specific subject, the more we understand that subject from God's perspective. As the verses are read together, they help shine a light on each other for a more accurate understanding of the topic. They also shine more light on our heart so that God can adjust us where we need to change as He draws us nearer to Himself.

Is that what your heart yearns for? Do you want to be closer to Him? Are you striving to be righteous in His eyes? Do you long to see Him face to face?

As you grow in your understanding of God's character and what He wants to develop in you, write it down in the form of a prayer in the space provided. Give it to Him. Make it personal. Be sincere.

### But wait, there's more...

We are not to only seek personal, spiritual growth. We must all start there – letting God change us and grow us. But if we only do that, we run the risk of being overly focused on ourselves. We also run the risk of missing out on one of the greatest joys of following Jesus.

Many moms have said, "Kids, you have to share!" When God opens our eyes to something cool, we should share it with someone else. As God teaches us, we should teach others.

When you do this, you are building up and edifying your brother or sister in Christ. If you are sharing your new insight with someone who has not yet put his or her faith in Jesus, then you are pointing that lost person toward Christ. Sharing what God is doing in your life is both an active way to love your neighbor and it is the best practice for learning how to make disciples.

*Intentionally making disciples for Jesus is the second part of our great adventure!*

We are called to love our neighbor, and we are called to make disciples. This requires both courage and faith.

May we be like strong, healthy trees: Rooted in love, grounded in truth, growing in faith, and bearing the fruit of righteousness. To fulfill our purpose and calling, our life must produce the fruit God designed it to bear. Remember, we cannot bear good fruit without good roots, and good roots are useless if the tree does not bear good fruit.

So let us always seek His face. Let us make sure we are spending intimate time with Him. May we humble ourselves before God every day. May we maintain an ever-maturing heart of love for Him, and then share that love with others.

Let the ADVENTURE begin!

# Day 1

## Knowing the God of the Gospel

*For God so loved the world that He gave His only begotten Son, that whoever believes in Him should not perish but have everlasting life.*

- John 3:16

The word "Gospel" means good news. And the good news of Jesus Christ is not complicated. In fact, Jesus Himself summed it up in just one sentence. His statement was so profound and comprehensive that it has become one of the most recognized and most quoted passages in the entire Bible. It is recorded for us here in the Book of John, chapter 3, verse 16.

To understand the Gospel message, we must understand the heart of God. God *is* love. That is His nature; that is His character. Everything God says and does is done within the context of divine love. And God loves *us*!

God loves us so much that He was willing to give up His only begotten Son in order to accomplish something amazing in us. He loves us so much that He chose to sacrifice His Son so that we would not perish in our sin and be cut off from Him for all eternity. Jesus willingly went to the cross and died in our place in order to demonstrate what love looks like. He loves us infinitely, and longs to give us an abundant life with Him, forever.

In case there was any confusion about exactly what Jesus did for us, Paul breaks it down and makes it crystal clear. "I declare to you the gospel which I preached to you, which also you received and in which you stand, by which also you are saved, if you hold fast that word which I preached to you – unless you believed in vain. For I delivered to you first of all that which I also received: that Christ died for our sins according to the Scriptures, and that He was buried, and that He rose again the third day according to the Scriptures" (1 Corinthians 15:1-4).

One of His closest disciples, Peter, also summed up the Gospel of Jesus in one sentence. He put it this way: [Jesus], "who Himself bore our sins in His own body on the tree, that we, having died to sins, might live for righteousness – by whose stripes you were healed" (1 Peter 2:24).

This is what we believe, this is how we live

righteous lives, and this is how we know God!

Through the death and resurrection of Jesus, God offers us the thorough forgiveness of all our sins. By placing our faith in Jesus Christ alone, He gives us eternal life. This Gospel, this good news, this Jesus, is the foundation and focus of our faith. Literally everything hinges on who Jesus is and what Jesus did.

There are many important doctrines in the Bible, but this one is the most critical. If we get too distracted from Jesus, we will become unfruitful for the Kingdom of God (John 15:5). If we try to get to God any other way, we will die in our sins (John 14:6). If we pervert this Gospel, the Apostle Paul says we will be accursed or eternally condemned (Galatians 1:6-9). If we rebel against our Creator and do not keep the faith, our name will be blotted out of the Book of Life and we will be cast into the lake of fire as punishment for our sins (Revelation 3:5 & 20:15).

Jesus stands at the crossroads of life and death and invites us to take the narrow road with Him. Let us therefore hold tightly to our faith in Jesus alone. Only His blood can wash away our sins. Only Jesus can save us from God's wrath. Only He can make us truly pure and right in God's eyes. Only Jesus can give us life that never ever ends.

Digging Deeper:    1 Corinthians 1:18 & 2:2.
2 Peter 3:9.   Acts 3:25-26.


My Prayer to my Father:

_____

_____

_____

_____

_____

I will share what I learned with: _____

# Day 2

## Words that Live and Cut

*For the word of God is living and powerful, and sharper than any two-edged sword, piercing even to the division of soul and spirit, and of joints and marrow, and is a discerner of the thoughts and intents of the heart.*

- Hebrews 4:12

How many times did Jesus have to defend the Scriptures? How many times did his apostles? Exactly none! The fact is the word of God is powerful enough to speak for itself. It is its own defense.

The Bible is not without historical validation. A great number of books and articles have been written that clearly show that the Bible is reliable, historically accurate, and trustworthy. But while the events recorded in the Bible take place in history, it was not *designed* to be merely academic.

5

It is, in fact, a *revelation*! God is transcendent. He is above us. The only way we know anything about Him is if He chooses to reveal it.

One of the main reasons for the Bible's longevity, and perhaps its most effective trait, is its power to reveal and expose. The Scriptures, enlivened by the Holy Spirit, work to rebuke our pride and selfishness and to draw us ever closer to God. It brings to light the evil thoughts and motives in our heart. It unreservedly addresses our shortcomings and faults.

By contrast, it speaks plainly about the glory and goodness of God. It tells of His wonderful works and His ways. It tells in brilliant detail the story of God's love for us, and how His great sacrifice reconciled us and brought us into a relationship with Him.

God's truth sets the standard for what is good and right – and reveals everything that falls short of that standard. After thousands of years, it is still powerful enough to pierce the heart and stir the soul.

Although God's truth is as global as human nature, different people react to it in different ways. If a person's heart is set on doing good, they may receive corrections and nudges with great joy. On the other hand, if they have hardened their heart against God, exposing their wrongdoings can generate immense bitterness or anger.

When Peter first preached on the day of Pentecost, those who heard him were "cut to the heart", or pierced, and asked what they needed to do (Acts 2:37). Even Paul (who was called Saul) kicked against the truth that poked at him for a while. Then his eyes were opened to the fact that Jesus is Lord (Acts 9:3-9).

Unfortunately, when forced to confront their sin, some will still turn violent. There are many people who hate spiritual light because their deeds are evil and they want to keep them hidden. When Peter and the others confronted the high priest and the council with the truth of Jesus, they were furious and plotted to kill them (Acts 5:27-33). To say they were furious or enraged misses a little of what the Greek word tries to convey. It could also be translated cut to the heart, rent with vexation, or sawn asunder (mentally). The truth of the Gospel had spiritually ripped them apart. It happened again after Stephen's speech in Acts 7:54. That is when they stoned him to death.

As God's children, we need to take His words to heart and integrate them into our lifestyle and speech. We need to let His word guide us, for His word is a lamp to our feet and a light to our path (Psalm 119:105). We need to allow ourselves to be set free by the truth of God's word. Jesus said that if we abide in His word we will truly be His disciples, and we will know the truth, the truth will set us free (John 8:31-32). When we allow the word of God to correct our motives and point us to Jesus, then our soul will find peace, and our heart will rejoice in God's presence.

The word of God is alive and powerfully effective. It discerns our thoughts and exposes the intentions of our heart. It judges between good and bad thoughts and distinguishes between good and bad motives. In other words, it is so sharp it can separate the spiritual from the physical and get to the heart of the matter - it shows us whether or not we are right with God.

With humility and perseverance, let us allow the word of God to change us from the inside out. And in turn, may we use His word to shine a light toward the people around us. When we do this in love, God's word will pierce their heart, expose their sins, and draw them to Christ.

Digging Deeper: Acts 4:29-30 & 6:8 - 7:60. Romans 10:17. Exodus 19:1 - 20:20.

My Prayer to my Father:

_____

_____

_____

_____

_____


I will share what I learned with: _____

# Day 3

## Self-Deception vs. Wisdom

*Let no one deceive himself. If anyone among you seems to be wise in this age, let him become a fool that he may become wise. For the wisdom of this world is foolishness with God. For it is written, "He catches the wise in their own craftiness"; and again, "The LORD knows the thoughts of the wise, that they are futile."*

- 1 Corinthians 3:18-20

How incredible is it to think that we actually have the ability to deceive ourselves! Others can deceive us by lying or misleading us, but how do we lie to ourselves? More importantly, *why* would we lie to ourselves?

Today, self-deception is more commonly referred to as self-justification.

Self-justification is the art of coming up with

excuses in order to justify behavior we know is wrong. Eventually our guilt subsides, our rationale takes root, and we begin to believe that our bad behavior is actually justified. The deception is that our thoughts and beliefs do not line up with God's truth.

Not only is it very easy to do, self-deception is extremely dangerous. Unless we are careful to guard against it, we often find ourselves consumed in our own little worlds. With our thoughts limited to those things that only concern us, we become quite eager to buy into ideas that are not in tune with the rest of reality. A person who is boastful or conceited about their achievements, ideas, or education is a thoroughly self-deceived person.

We deceive ourselves into thinking we are smarter than we really are. Worse still, it is not a big leap for many "smart" people to think they are smarter than God. Of course it is not usually vocalized that bluntly, but that is really at the heart of the matter when we take issue at how God runs the universe or blame Him when He allows something we do not like. We may not understand it, but that does not mean that God is wrong.

We must keep our hearts and minds in check. We need to be reminded of the wisdom, knowledge, and truth of God. Compared to His omniscience, our deepest wisdom is but foolishness, and our most profound thoughts are vain and empty. Like an ant who knows only about the leaf he crawls on and the community he exists within, our perspective of the universe and the world we live in is remarkably limited. When Job searched the extremities of his knowledge for an explanation of his perils, God answered him, "Where were you when I laid the foundations of the earth? Tell Me, if you have understanding" (Job 38:4). We can only see what is in front of us. We cannot grasp the big picture unless God reveals it.

Earlier in this letter to the Corinthian Christians, Paul says, "God has chosen the foolish things of the world to put to shame the wise" (1 Corinthians 1:27). This is particularly applicable to our salvation. "For the message of the cross is foolishness to those who are perishing, but to us who are being saved it is the power of God" (1:18).

Everyone wants to think that they are wise, but where does real wisdom come from? The Bible says that "the fear of the LORD is the beginning of wisdom, and the knowledge of the Holy One is understanding" (Proverbs 9:10). What then is the distinction between God's wisdom and man's wisdom? I believe the difference is in the *perspective* as well as the *purpose*.

God alone has the proper perspective. God sees how *all* things affect each other; all we can see is how a few things affect *us*. We need to be willing to recognize that God has a grand plan, and that we can only perceive a tiny fraction of it.

Purposes and motives also distinguish between man's wisdom and God's wisdom. Man's selfish idea of "get what you can, while you can," is in sharp contrast to God's concept of "it is more blessed to give than to receive" (Acts 20:35). God's wisdom is rooted in His generous, limitless love; man's wisdom is based on his selfish, limitless pride.

Our pride is what leads us into self-deception. We seem to naturally think of ourselves more highly than we should. We also tend to minimize and justify the wrong things we do, even as we point out the faults in others.

Only when we are honest with God and ourselves can we discover true humility. The obvious benefit of humility is that we are able to glorify and exalt God with clarity, sincerity, and without arrogance. Also, God greets our humility with grace, for "God resists the proud, but gives grace to the humble" (1 Peter 5:5).

To glory in our own wisdom is foolishness. Let us be honest with ourselves and recognize how limited we are. Let us acknowledge God's unlimited knowledge, power, and goodness. Let us be willing to look foolish in the eyes of the world as we pursue true wisdom from God.

Digging Deeper:    Isaiah 55:8-9.   Galatians 6:3.
1 Timothy 6:20-21.   1 Corinthians 1:18-31.


My Prayer to my Father:

_____

_____

_____

_____

_____


I will share what I learned with: _____

# Day 4

## Get a Life

*For whoever desires to save his life will lose it, but whoever loses his life for My sake will find it.*

- Matthew 16:25

The contrasts of this statement are out-shined only by its irony. From the beginning, we humans have sought our own purposes, and our main goal has always been to protect our most valuable resource: our own life. Even though we know that death is inevitable, we try to avoid it for as long as possible.

Jesus wants to give us life. In fact, the whole reason He came was to save us. The scandalous part about following Jesus is that He requires us to lay down our life and give it over to Him. He pits everything the world has to offer against what He has to offer. We can either pursue our own ways or we can pursue Him. We cannot do both.

Jesus is blunt about the vanity of worldly pursuits, and their consequences. He is also rather explicit about the personal sacrifice He requires from us. He tells us to count the cost of being His disciple. If we are really going to follow Him, we must be willing to give up everything, even our life, for His sake.

To avoid any confusion, His follow up statements offer a bit of clarity. In regards to those who vainly try to save their own life, Jesus poses a couple of deeply introspective questions. Almost rhetorically he asks, "For what profit is it to a man if he gains the whole world, and loses his own soul?" Taking it a step further and making it a little more personal, He adds, "What shall a man give in exchange for his soul?" (vs. 26) If we were to lose it, what would we do or what would we pay to get our soul back?

If the question is, "What is more important than protecting our soul?" then the obvious answer is, "Nothing!" Even if you could be Emperor of the World from this very moment until the day you died, would it be worth eternity? Would a few years of feeling like you possessed unlimited power and infinite wealth be worth being lost forever?

Sadly, despite the inherent and immeasurable value of our soul, many people pawn it away for fools-gold.

So, how do we find real life? How do we

acquire the eternal life that Jesus offers? How exactly do we "lose our life for His sake?" In verse 24, Jesus says, "Let him deny himself, and take up his cross, and follow Me."

Humble submission is the first part of the process. We must willingly place ourselves under His lordship. We are to deny ourselves repeatedly in order to give ourselves completely to the One who loves us infinitely.

The second part of losing our life for His sake is taking up our cross. In the days of Jesus, the cross was a common means of Roman execution. When Jesus first told His disciples to take up their cross and follow Him, they must have thought He was out of His mind. They knew what a Roman cross was, and it did not conjure up pleasant mental images.

Think about it. They did not have our post-resurrection perspective. Jesus himself had not died on the cross yet, so they did not have Jesus' example to follow. To them, the cross was not a religious relic or a piece of diamond-studded jewelry. Their *only* mental picture was that of a gruesome, bloody, painful death.

Today, you and I can see the bigger picture. With our privileged hindsight, we understand that when Jesus was carrying His cross, He was laying down His life for us.

But sometimes this "bigger picture" view blinds us to what Jesus is really saying here. When we hear the words *cross* or *crucifixion,* we immediately focus on Jesus' experience rather than our own personal application. Make no mistake, He was asking His disciples, and us, to literally lay down our lives for Him, day in and day out, through good times and bad.

To actually die and be a martyr for Jesus is a one-time deal, though. While we need to be willing to do that, He is asking for more than that. We are to take up our cross *daily.* That means a complete surrendering to the will of God every moment of our life. Every day is a new opportunity to humbly set aside what we want and do what He wants, go where He wants, and say what He wants. Our life is not about us anymore.

The last piece of this puzzle, and the key to eternal life, is simple: Follow Jesus. He gave this personal invitation to many of His disciples, saying, "Come, follow me" (Matthew 4:19; Mark 2:14; John 1:43). He now desires the same, deep relationship with us. Jesus holds out His hand, looks us in the eyes, smiles, and says, "Follow me."

Let us establish Him as Emperor, King, Ruler, and Master over our lives. Let us sacrifice the temporary on the alter of the eternal. Let us lay down our desires and follow His will. Let us follow Him with our own cross, rejoicing when we are counted worthy to suffer shame for His name (Acts 5:41). Remember, we are not just losing our life;

we are losing our life *for Jesus*. And Jesus *is* life!

Digging Deeper:    John 12:24-26 & 17:3.   Luke 14:27-33.

My Prayer to my Father:

_____

_____

_____

_____

_____

I will share what I learned with: _____

# Day 5

## The One and Only

*Jesus said to him, I am the way, the truth, and the life. No one comes to the Father except through Me.*

- John 14:6

In a world filled with countless religions, many people ponder their accuracy. Each one promotes its own ideas and encourages a lifestyle that is consistent with its beliefs. With each religion claiming to be the only way, how can we determine which one really is the right way?

Many people are looking for something more fulfilling than what they already have. They are searching for a religion that "works for them." Unfortunately, they seem to be more concerned with achieving a state of happiness than finding the truth.

Every religion claims to provide the keys to a good and meaningful life. They also offer something better in the afterlife. *But which one actually works?* Which religion makes good on its promise to provide an abundant life here, and gives its devotees confidence in facing the next life?

Almost all of them trace their beginning back to a prophet or enlightened individual. The Buddhists have Gautama Buddha, Muslims have Muhammad, Mormons have Joseph Smith, and the Jews have a series of prophets like Abraham and Moses.

While Christians also trace their beginning back to a single individual named Jesus, there are some critical distinctions.

The other prophets claimed to know and speak the truth, yet they were all born and eventually died like everyone else. But Jesus is unique; He is different from all of the other religious leaders. He was not born like everyone else; He was given birth by a virgin. During His life, He did many miracles, healed many sick people, and fulfilled many prophecies. While His death was a critical part of His mission, one of the things that set Him apart from everyone else is the fact that He rose from the dead.

Then there were His outlandish claims! With one sweeping statement, Jesus made the ultimate exclusive declaration. While others have claimed to know the way, Jesus claimed to *be* the way. While they claimed to have found the truth, He claimed to *be* the truth. Furthermore, while they claimed to have the keys to real life, He claimed to *be* life.

While the followers of all other religions can be very sincere and very devout, almost all of them lack two key things. First, they lack confidence in their current purity. Second, they lack confidence in their eternal destiny.

The followers of Jesus are very different. Christianity the only religious group that is filled with people that are *fully convinced* they have been made right in God's eyes, and that they will spend eternity with Him.

Jesus is the way. Many people who try to make their own path end up more lost than when they started. We must go through Jesus to get to the Father. No philosophy, no rituals, no empty traditions, and no other person can make us into who we need to be or get us where we need to go.

Jesus is the truth. To deviate from Him is to be deceived. To believe anything that contradicts His words is to believe a lie. Paul issues a dire warning to those that would try to lead people away from Jesus. He says, "If anyone preaches any other gospel to you than what you have received, let him be accursed" (Galatians 1:9).

Jesus is life. John 1:3-4 states, "All things were made through Him, and without Him nothing was made that was made. In Him was life, and the life was the light of men." To complete the picture, Jesus also shows His power over death. In John 11:25-26, Jesus says, "I am the resurrection and the life. He who believes in Me, though he may die, he shall live. And whoever lives and believes in Me shall never die. Do you believe this?" He then revealed His resurrection power by shouting, "Lazarus, come forth!" And Lazarus, who had been dead for four days, walked out of his tomb! (vs. 43-44)

While being questioned by the religious rulers, Peter made it clear that there is no salvation except through Jesus, "for there is no other name under heaven given among men by which we must be saved" (Acts 4:12). We cannot build our own stairway to heaven, and God will not allow our pride to come into His presence.

In His infinite wisdom, He has crafted a perfect path. Since God is the ultimate source of truth, His path requires that we actually trust Him. Coming to God is not about joining a church, saying a prayer, or keeping rules; it is simply and completely believing what He says.

God's perfect plan excludes all forms of pride and selfishness. We do not need God's help to maintain a tradition, to give money to a worthy cause, or to try to live a "better" life than some other random person. These, and a thousand other religious things, may only puff us up in pride.

We must all place our faith in who Jesus is and what He did for us. God has decided to offer salvation to us as a free gift through His Son. Therefore, to reject the gift is to reject the Giver.

To come to God, we must come to Him His way. To experience the love and forgiveness of the Father and be assured of eternal life with Him, we must follow Jesus. To pursue any other path is to put our faith in ourselves, and put our confidence in our own ability to keep the rules.

We must believe in Jesus, and we must follow Him wholeheartedly. For Jesus Christ is the only one who can make us right with the Father.

Let us follow the Way sincerely and whole-heartedly; let us know the Truth intimately; and let us live in His abundant, eternal Life by letting His abundant, eternal Life live in us.

Digging Deeper: Luke 10:16, 21-22. Matthew 7:13-29. John 8.

My Prayer to my Father:

_____

_____

_____

_____

_____

I will share what I learned with: _____

# Day 6

## Reconcile and Repeat

*Now all things are of God, who has reconciled us to Himself through Jesus Christ, and has given us the ministry of reconciliation, that is, that God was in Christ reconciling the world to Himself, not imputing their trespasses to them, and has committed to us the word of reconciliation.*

- 2 Corinthians 5:18-19

As believers in Christ, we have experienced divine reconciliation. Through a wide variety of circumstances, we have come to the awareness of our deep need for God. Although our prayers may have been different, something inside of us changed when we finally surrendered ourselves to God and put our trust in Jesus. A simple, but profound thing happened: we went from being enemies of God to being reconciled to God.

29

God has always desired an intimate relationship with us. Even while we took pleasure in doing things that displeased Him, He was already planning ways to draw us back. When we were running from Him, He was eagerly waiting for our return. Through Jesus, our relationship with our Creator was made right. Like the prodigal son, He welcomed us back with open arms and a joyous celebration.

This miracle was made possible when Jesus came to die on a cross for us. By doing this, He provided an acceptable sacrifice so that we might be forgiven for our lawlessness and rebellion. Through a simple, yet sincere faith in Jesus and what He did, we are ushered into a deep, loving relationship with God that will never end.

Having brought us into His family, He then commits to us the ministry of reconciliation. We are now His servants; we are on His team; we are living for His cause. God wants to use us in His continued effort to draw people to Himself. Even as God used others to point and guide us toward Him, He now calls us to be light in a dark world, pointing others to Jesus.

God gives us a joy and confidence that is different than anything this world could give. With this inner assurance of His acceptance, we can boldly step out and offer this gift of love to those who do not know Him. As our affection for God grows, so should our love for others.

A practical place to begin our reconciliation ministry is on our knees. As we begin to pray for family members, friends, co-workers, and neighbors, two powerful things begin to happen. First, God hears our prayers and begins to work in their hearts, drawing them to Himself. Secondly, God begins to work in us, increasing our capacity to love, opening our eyes for opportunities to share, and causing us to genuinely want others to have what God has given us.

There is an emotional aspect to this too. If you hear of someone in a foreign country experiencing a miracle of God and becoming a Christian, you may thank God for that soul, but your emotional response might be minimal. On the other hand, if you intercede for a neighbor for years and play a part in their conversion, you will be emotionally invested in them and will rejoice with the angels!

Out of our love toward God, let us begin to reach out and offer His divine grace to others. Remember, whether we do the planting, watering, or reaping, it is God who brings the spiritual increase. Jesus Christ alone is the redeemer of souls. He has called us to be His faithful servants and ministers. Let us do our part in reconciling the world to God by loving them and pointing them to Christ.

Make no mistake, this is a vital part of the

kingdom of God. And we are the King's ambassadors.

Digging Deeper: Matthew 4:17-20 & 28:16-20. Mark 6:7-13. Luke 10:1-20. Hebrews 4:14-16 & 10:19-22.

My Prayer to my Father:

_____

_____

_____

_____

_____

I will share what I learned with: _____

# Day 7

## Better than Me?

*Let nothing be done through selfish ambition or conceit, but in lowliness of mind let each esteem others better than himself.*

- Philippians 2:3

God's ways are not our ways. There are few areas in life where this is more evident than in our relationships with other people. Whether it is in a rat race at work or a power struggle in a marriage, God has called us to a new way of thinking. God has shown us a divine way of loving.

The simple principle taught in this passage is humility. This "lowliness of mind" is contrasted with its eternal enemy: pride. Paul was encouraging the Christians in Philippi to shun a life of self-exaltation, and to pursue a humility that would actually lift others up.

There is a natural tendency in us to fight for what we think we deserve. We may put others down in order to get ahead. We may boast of our accomplishments in order to receive recognition, power, or position. We may even be tempted to sue someone for personal gain. The tragic result is that people are often hurt in the wake of our ambition. Even if we achieve financial success, even if the other person "recovers", we are likely to have caused significant hurt to a human being that God treasures. We will have damaged a relationship that should have been defined by love.

When we steal the spotlight, we are stepping over others in order to promote our own glory. Not only is this the opposite of how God wants us to love people, it actually becomes a hindrance to what God wants to do in their life.

We are to value people as God does. He has called us to closely guard our relationships, for it is through this avenue that we express God's love to others.

Jesus set the example for us. Although He was God, He humbled Himself and took on the form of a human servant, becoming obedient to the Father, even to the point of death (Philippians 2:5-8). These were the facts on the ground, but don't forget the bigger picture. Jesus was motivated by a divine love. His whole purpose was to reconcile mankind to God.

God has called us to this same lifestyle of love. More than an abstract idea, we are given His example, as well as practical applications for this principle. To aid us in our effort to please the Father, we are offered a solution to our selfishness: viewing others higher than ourselves.

This is a choice we make, but it is not easy and it is not natural. Our sinful nature wants us to be the center of the universe. Our pride strives to set ourselves over others, even if we have to tear them down to get there. In a group of people, we want to be first. We want to be number one.

Jesus is the cure! When we deny ourselves, take up our cross, and follow Him, He gives us the strength and mindset to put others first. Even more importantly, He will change our heart so that we do it for the right reasons. God wants us to walk in humility so that we can truly love others. He also wants us to be a light that draws them to Jesus. Then Jesus can reconcile them to the Father and give them eternal life.

We were all created by an all-powerful God; we were all formed in His image. Without a doubt, everyone is of equal value in the eyes of God. His intense love for all of us was clearly revealed in the life and works of Jesus Christ, whose death on the cross proved our worth, and whose resurrection from the dead gives us assurance of eternal life. Now He wants us to reflect divine love by putting other people first and esteeming them higher than ourselves.

As we follow Jesus Christ, let us adapt His mindset. He did not come to be served, but to serve (Mark 10:45). Let us then put away our pride, our lust, our fighting, and our envy. Let us choose instead to serve others and build them up. Let us live out God's divine love by walking in humility and encouraging others toward the kingdom of God.

Digging Deeper:    John 13:34-35 & 15:12-13.
1 Corinthians 3:2-8.

My Prayer to my Father:

_____

_____

_____

_____

_____

I will share what I learned with: _____

# Day 8

## Absolutely Positively Shalt Not

*You shall have no other gods before Me.*

- Exodus 20:3

God communicated these words after He had just delivered the Israelites out of Egypt. Through His deliverance, God had purposely shown Himself to be far greater than the gods that were worshipped by the Egyptians. For example, they worshipped the sun god, Ra, and God brought a darkness so thick that it could be felt (Exodus 10:21). God made it known that he was strong and mighty, as well as gracious and merciful. He left no doubt that He was indeed the one, true, and living God.

He took this time alone with them in the wilderness to show them His glory and teach them His laws. He wanted them to trust Him, to obey Him, and to worship Him alone. A covenant was formed, and they became God's people, and the He became their God.

By revealing Himself, God set the Israelites apart and made them His own. The God they served now defined their identity. He was going to make them a nation of priests that would serve Him alone.

As the only nation consecrated to God as a whole, He wanted them to set the example of righteous living. God's presence and name would dwell among them, and by them God would draw the world to Himself.

Through their rituals and sacrifices, He made a distinction between things that are holy and things that are common. Through their prophets, He would foretell of things to come. Through their lineage, He would give the world a Savior.

The phrase "before me" in this verse gives the impression of "above me" or "preeminence over me." While this is certainly the case, this definition can be deepened by adding to it the idea of "in front of me" or "in my sight." God, in His wisdom, was preparing his chosen people for what was to lie ahead. He was leading them toward the land that He had promised to Abraham and his descendants. Although it was a land flowing with milk and honey, it was also a land flooded with idolatry. He did not want them deceived and led astray to worship false gods.

God was jealous for their attention and their

affection. They were to worship Him above all other gods, and they were to worship Him alone.

Unfortunately, they did not keep this command. But neither did they just wake up one day and decide to worship gods they had never heard of. It started when they disobeyed God and compromised with surrounding nations. Over time, the Israelites allowed the subtle deceptions and false ideas of those ungodly nations to creep into their own society.

Through Jesus Christ, God establishes a covenant with all of us who believe in Him. He adopts us into His family and makes us His own. He even calls us His children. In this dynamic relationship, the old command still applies to us. We are to worship Him alone, and we are to serve Him above all else.

Today, our challenge is similar. We are bombarded with false teachings about Jesus on one side and confronted with an anti-God, secular worldview on the other. There are many paths that claim to lead to heaven, but only one will actually get us there.

May we not allow ourselves to be deceived by false concepts of God. May we not be distracted by the greed and lusts of this world. May we have no other gods before Him. Therefore, let us commit ourselves to the one true God, and determine to love Him with all of our heart, with all of our thoughts, and with everything we set our hands to do.

Digging Deeper:    John 14:1-11.   Matthew 12:30.
Joshua 24:14-18.

My Prayer to my Father:

_____

_____

_____

_____

_____

I will share what I learned with: _____

# Day 9

## Believing Lies

*The coming of the lawless one is according to the working of Satan, with all power, signs, and lying wonders, and with all unrighteous deception among those who perish, because they did not receive the love of the truth, that they might be saved. And for this reason God will send them strong delusion, that they should believe the lie.*

-2 Thessalonians 2:9-11

Although this is a detailed but brief glimpse into the power and workings of the "son of perdition", it also gives a telling description of the people that will follow him.

Satan will have amazing powers to deceive, and he will use these supernatural signs and wonders to lead astray all those who do not love the truth. His miracles will impress and deceive many.

Those people will not seek out what is good, cling to what is right, or love what is true. This is their error and their downfall. In verse 12, it says that they rejected the truth because they took pleasure in unrighteousness. They searched for fun and not for truth. Paul describes this kind of person perfectly in 2 Timothy 3:4 when he talks about those who are "lovers of pleasure rather than lovers of God."

The temptation to pursue pleasure instead of God is strong. Many people put God on the back burner because He would interfere with their life-style. Even a lot of people who claim to believe in God have made Him a very low priority in their everyday life.

The people who are rejecting God now in order to pursue the temporary joys of this life are already self-deceived. They try to do away with truth by claiming that it is unknowable or relative. The bottom line is this, if they do not love and desire truth now, they will be completely deceived when the "man of sin" comes in his power.

How can we avoid believing lies? How can we escape strong delusion? How do we keep ourselves from the deceptions of unrighteousness? How might we be saved?

First, we should receive the love of the truth. Secondly, we should abhor what is evil and cling to what is good (Romans 12:9).

It has been said that the best way to recognize a counterfeit dollar bill is to become very familiar with a real one. Likewise, the best way to recognize a lie is to know the truth. John starts off his Gospel with the phrase, "In the beginning was the Word, and the Word was with God, and the Word was God" (1:1). In John 17:17, it says that God's word is truth. Jesus also makes a profoundly comprehensive statement in John 14:6 when He says, "I am the way, the truth, and the life. No one comes to the Father except through Me."

Note how all three fit together. God's Word is truth; Jesus is God's Word; Jesus is truth. Jesus is the personification of all that is true. We cannot get to heaven without receiving God's truth, His Word, and His Son.

Too many people shun God's Word. They refuse to let Jesus have any part in their life. Sadly, in the end, God will give them over to their selfish desires and they will thoroughly believe the lies.

As followers of Jesus Christ, may we be honest with our selves and our priorities. Let us desperately seek to know that which is real and good and true. Let us determine in our hearts to take hold of the truth and never let Him go.

Digging Deeper:    2 Timothy 4:1-5.   Mark 12:29-31.
Revelation 2:4-5.


My Prayer to my Father:

_____

_____

_____

_____

_____


I will share what I learned with: _____

# Day 10

## Ignorantly Self-Righteous

*For they being ignorant of God's righteousness, and seeking to establish their own righteousness, have not submitted to the righteousness of God.*

- Romans 10:3

It is not possible for everyone to be right. It would defy logic and observable reality. Some people would disagree, saying, "But there are so many different religions out there, and they all contain some good teachings, why can't they all be paths to the same God?" The answer is easy: because they contradict each other. Why would a transcendent being tell one group that he is the single Creator of all that exists, and then lead another group to believe that there are a multitude of gods? That would only produce confusion and doubt.

All of creation sings of a brilliantly designed

origin. And this Originator has not left us without hope of knowing Him. On the contrary, knowing Him was His intention from the beginning.

A supposed lack of information and evidence is not the problem. The issue is how we handle what we have been given. Too often, people choose to ignore God's self-revelation and instruction, searching instead for a spiritual path that better suites their own desires. They want to think that they are a good person, but they want to be good *their way*. Thus the conflict arises between their way and God's way.

We cannot come to God sincerely if we refuse to approach Him in the way that He has planned and prepared. God is holy, and He has established a perfect plan for sinful, selfish people like us to be adequately purified so that we can stand in His presence. To shun His sole offer of salvation is to demonstrate that we do not believe what He has said. It is actually an act of rebellion against our Creator.

We must ask ourselves some tough questions: How important is truth to us? What are we willing to sacrifice in order to find it? Are we willing to cling to God and His truth, no matter what the cost?

The righteousness (goodness, right-standing) that God gives is different than our righteousness. We can try to be "religious" or "spiritual"; we can do it through an organized religion or we can float around and be led only by our feelings; but if we are not being righteous *God's way*, we are being "self-righteous"!

When God looks at us, does He see His righteousness in us, or does He see us covered in our own righteousness? True righteousness, or right-standing before God, comes from God alone, for it is only His to give. We cannot earn it or create some for ourselves. It is given when we place our faith in what He has accomplished for us.

We are made righteous when we place our trust in Jesus Christ and His sacrificial death for our sins. This is when we deny ourselves and submit our lives to His lordship. That is it. Nothing more, nothing less. And when we fall and mess up, we go right back to the cross.

This submission is the hard part of the equation for many of us. Its difficulty lies in its requisite humility and self-denial. It goes against our selfish nature, which wants to be in control and bend all things to our own pleasure. Ultimately, it is our pride that keeps us from finding peace with God.

We need to be honest with ourselves. Are we being spiritual God's way, or are we indulging in a self-made religious fantasy? Are we creating our own path, or are we submitting ourselves to the one that God has laid out in the person of Jesus Christ?

Please understand, you can still insist on doing it your way. You can step up to the buffet of religions and pick and choose what you like, just do not expect to leave full.

Only by submitting to the righteousness of God is our conscience cleansed and our joy made full. Let us take the time to learn God's ways. Let us be honest with our behavior and sincere in our motives. If pleasing God is really our ultimate goal, then let us lay our lives at His feet and do what He says.

Digging Deeper:    1 Peter 2:24.    2 Timothy 3:16-17. 2 Corinthians 5:17-21.

My Prayer to my Father:

_____

_____

_____

_____

_____

I will share what I learned with: _____

# Day 11

## God Gives Perfect Gifts

*Every good gift and every perfect gift is from above, and comes down from the Father of lights, with whom is no variation or shadow of turning.*

- James 1:17

It is so easy to want to blame God when things go wrong, but how often do we give Him credit when things are going well? The Scripture is clear: if it is good or perfect, it is a gift from God. He is eternal and unchanging, and like His knowledge and power, His love and His kindness are infinite.

God takes great delight in giving us good things. But that does not mean we will always have a pleasant life. In the book of Job, God allowed Satan to take away everything that Job had. God was not being mean, for He knew that once He revealed Himself to Job, everything would be put into a proper, eternal perspective. Job's only shortcoming through the ordeal was that when he was accused of sin he defended his own goodness instead of God's sovereignty. But at no point in his hardship did he deny or turn his back on God. Once Job's faithfulness was proven, God blessed him and gave him twice as much as he had before. This is not a formula for financial success; it is a formula for spiritual growth!

Without giving Satan undue attention, we need to understand that his ultimate goal is to turn our hearts against God. Satan hunts us down like a lion; he wants to sift us like wheat. He comes to steal and kill and destroy, and he is good at it! He loves to crush and pervert God's gifts. He accuses God of not being good, but he is a liar, for God cannot be anything but good.

It is during these trials that our hearts are tested. Which do we love more, the gifts or the Giver?

We came into this world with nothing, and we will take nothing with us when we leave. Everything that we acquire while we are here is a gift from God.

Our families and our friends are a gift. Our homes, our jobs, every penny we will ever earn or be given is a present from the Father. Even our talents and skills come from Him.

In Matthew 7:9-11, Jesus illustrates the Father's generous heart. He points out that if a man's son were to ask for bread, he would not give him a stone. And if the son asks for fish, the father would not give him a serpent. If evil men can give good things to their children, how much more will God give good things to those who ask?

But what about the *perfect* gifts? For that we have to look beyond the material things. God is not just great and good; He is the greatest and the best. Thus the greatest thing God could give us is Himself.

God has given us His perfect Word from the beginning of time that we might know Him as the Creator and Sustainer of life. God has given us His perfect Son, Jesus Christ, that through Him we might be forgiven of our sins and inherit eternal life.

God has also given us His perfect Holy Spirit. His Spirit then provides us with a wide variety of spiritual gifts that enable us to glorify and exalt our Creator. The Holy Spirit gives us the strength to resist temptation and live for God. He also gives us the supernatural power to be a witness of what Jesus has done.

All good things come from God. There is no good thing that we possess that is not a gift from above. So let us continually give thanks to Him who is from everlasting to everlasting, and who is the same yesterday, today and forever, for He is good, and He is perfect.

Digging Deeper:    Matthew 6:25-30 & 16:19.    Luke 12:32.    John 16:23-24.


My Prayer to my Father:

_____

_____

_____

_____

_____


I will share what I learned with: _____

# Day 12

## Beauty and Rust

*Do not lay up for yourselves treasures on earth, where moth and rust destroy and where thieves break in and steal.*

- Matthew 6:19

Television commercials call out to us, and billboards paint a pretty picture. Supermodels entice us to buy their products, and neighbors make us jealous with their expensive toys. But Jesus has a clear warning for us. We are not to be greedy for worldly things or distracted by the accumulation of them.

Summing up the concepts of vanity, covetousness, and what is really important, Jesus admonishes us to store up treasures for ourselves in heaven and not here on earth. What we invest toward our heavenly goal can never be taken away, but what we accumulate here and now will most certainly be taken from us sooner or later. The famous missionary, Jim Elliot, once said, "He is no fool who gives what he cannot keep to gain what he cannot lose."[1]

Where we spend our time, energy, and money will determine where our loyalties lie. These are excellent indicators that bring to light what we are passionate about and what we consider priorities. If you want to know what is *really* important to you, take a step back and look at how you spend your time and where you spend your money.

In Exodus 20:17, God gave Moses and the Israelites a commandment: "You shall not covet... anything that is thy neighbor's." In Luke 12:15, Jesus warns a man about coveting even his own rightful inheritance. To illustrate the importance of correct priorities, he tells the story of a rich man who was making plans to save up enough of his wealth to live comfortably for the next few years. When God required his soul that night, it exposed his shortsightedness and selfishness. The man was saving up wealth for himself, but he was not rich toward God.

Covetousness is an expression of selfishness. It is a lust that can never be satisfied. It seeks to draw attention to us rather than to God. Ultimately, it reveals a lack of trust in Him as a provider, and can even be a vain attempt to replace spiritual intimacy with material things.

Wanting things too much destroys relationships. And relationships are a priority for God. Couples argue over finances, families split over inheritances, and countless lawsuits are filed because someone did not get what they thought they deserved. Love seeks to restore relationships, coveting seeks money and things at the expense of relationships.

Running counter to our pride, most of our heavenly treasures are stored secretly. They are accumulated very subtly. Sure, you can store up heavenly treasures by being involved at church, giving to ministries, and supporting missionaries, but most of our godly riches will come from our day-to-day lifestyle. If building God's kingdom is a priority, then we will be praying for our family members and co-workers. We will forgive people when they lie to us. We will readily give to those in need. And we will tell others what Jesus has done for us.

We do not always have to wait to enjoy our treasures however. There is great satisfaction in visiting people who are in jail or in the hospital. If we are earnestly interceding for people, then we will be able to truly rejoice with them when God works a miracle in their life or touches their heart in a special way. If you love people enough to tell them about Jesus, there is almost nothing that can surpass the sheer joy of seeing someone come into a new life by placing their faith in Him!

We should lay ourselves before God's presence and ask: "Am I trying to glorify You and expand Your Kingdom, or exalt myself with luxury goods and brand name items?" "Am I working for Your pleasure or my own?" "Do I love You more than I love the things in this world?"

In reality, everything belongs to God. Things are not evil, and having things is not a sin. The problem is when we want things too much. The Bible does *not* say that money is the root of all evil; it says the *love of money* is the problem (1 Timothy 6:10). We cannot let materialism take priority over loving God and loving others.

Let us fix our eyes and hearts on the Lord of all creation, and guard against our tendency to covet worldly things. Let us seek first the kingdom of God and His righteousness, and then trust Him for everything else. When we use our things for God's glory, they become beautiful. This kind of investment cannot be stolen and will not rust away. When we spend our lives leading others to trust in Jesus, that is a treasure that will last forever.

Digging Deeper:    Matthew 6 & 13:3-23.  Luke 16:9-13.

My Prayer to my Father:

_____

_____

_____

_____

_____

I will share what I learned with: _____

[1] Jim Elliot Quotes. (n.d.). BrainyQuote.com. Retrieved September 19, 2020, from BrainyQuote.com Website: https://www.brainyquote.com/quotes/jim_elliot_189244

# Day 13

## Strange Fire Meets Holy Fire

*Nadab and Abihu, the sons of Aaron, each took his censer and put fire in it, put incense on it, and offered profane fire before the LORD, which He had not commanded them. So fire went out from the LORD and devoured them, and they died before the LORD.*

- Leviticus 10:1-2

God had blasted the land of Egypt with ten different plagues in order to free His people. He parted the Red Sea in order to deliver them from the pursuing army. Why was He now destroying two of His newly appointed priests?

God had just established, in incredible detail, exactly how He was to be worshipped. When everything was set in order, Moses and Aaron came out of the tabernacle of the congregation and blessed the people. At that point, fire came out from before the Lord and consumed the burnt offering, which was on the altar. Seeing this absolutely spectacular display of power, Nadab and Abihu decided to take matters into their own hands.

At first glance, their death by fire may seem quite harsh. Why would God do this? Why such a severe punishment?

Moses gave the answer to Aaron, who was their father and also the high priest. God had spoken to him and said, "By those who come near Me I must be regarded as holy; and before all the people I must be glorified" (vs. 3). A similar sentiment is expressed in chapter 22, verse 32, when God said, "You shall not profane My holy name, but I will be hallowed among the children of Israel. I am the LORD who sanctifies you." We are to regard God as holy, and He is the one who makes us holy.

Later, King Saul did something similar and it cost him the crown. When he was supposed to destroy the Amalekites and their flocks, he kept the best of the sheep and oxen for sacrifices to God. Samuel, the prophet, rebuked him saying, "Has the LORD as great delight in burnt offerings and sacrifices, as in obeying the voice of the LORD? Behold, to obey is better than sacrifice, and to heed than the fat of rams. For rebellion is as the sin of witchcraft, and stubbornness is as iniquity and idolatry. Because you have rejected the word of the

LORD, He also has rejected you from being king" (1 Samuel 15:22-23).

God is still the same today. He is not so much concerned with our religious activities and traditions as He is with our loyalty and obedience. These are the true tests of our love for Him.

Many people seem to either fear God for His wrath or love Him like a daddy. The reality is, we need to do both. We must revere God and regard Him as holy, knowing that no uncleanness or sin can stand before Him. We must also wrap our brains around the fact that He loves us lavishly and wants us to be with Him.

Psalms 111:10 says that the fear of the Lord is the beginning of wisdom. Yet Hebrews 4:6 admonishes us to come boldly to the throne of grace. The more we understand His glory and righteousness, the more we are in awe of Him. The more we understand what we have been saved from, the more we love Him.

Today, just as in the time of Nadab and Abihu, God has specifically revealed how He is to be worshipped. We are not free to pick and choose how we want to do it. We worship His way, or we worship in vain.

Jesus Christ is that way. He is the truth and he is the life (John 14:6). If we refuse to submit to His lordship throughout the week, then our Sunday worship begins to smell like "strange fire" (KJV translation). If our faith rests in anything other than the sufficiency of Jesus, then we are offering the sacrifices of rebellion. If we reject the Word of God, then He will reject us.

Let us offer the Lord of all creation a sweet smelling sacrifice of praise. Let us worship Him in spirit, and let us worship Him in truth.

Digging Deeper:    Acts 5:1-11.    Matthew 25:31-46.

My Prayer to my Father:

_____

_____

_____

_____

_____

I will share what I learned with: _____

# Day 14

## The Great Escape

*No temptation has overtaken you except such as is common to man; but God is faithful, who will not allow you to be tempted beyond what you are able, but with the temptation will also make the way of escape, that you may be able to bear it.*

- 1 Corinthians 10:13

Solomon's old adage that there is nothing new under the sun (Ecclesiastes 1:9) can also be applied to our moral lives today. The same things that we struggle with now, Solomon struggled with thousands of years ago. That which tempts us has tempted countless others before us. The things we deal with now, our grandchildren will also confront.

The Ten Commandments are timeless because human temptation does not change or go away. Sinful human nature is common to all people. So whether we are enticed by others or whether we are led away by our own lusts, we can find hope in the fact that there is always a way out.

Through it all, God is consistent. He remains faithful, even when we are not.

To state the obvious, God does *not* want us to sin. He wants us to be pure so that we can honor and glorify Him. When He makes us clean, we are able to enjoy Him (and life) to the fullest.

In his letter to the Christians in Corinth, Paul describes two specific ways in which God's faithfulness to us is demonstrated. First of all, God is sovereign and will not *allow* us to be tempted beyond what we are able to bear. God knows where our limits are, but more importantly, He knows that His power is not limited. The fact is that when we put our faith in Jesus, we can do all things through Him, for He strengthens us (Philippians 4:13).

Secondly, God is merciful and will provide a way of *escape* in every temptation. It could result from an accountability relationship with a close friend, one last chance to walk away from a situation, a nudge in your spirit saying, "don't do that," or any number of other methods, but there is always a way to avoid sin. If our hearts are right, we will be on the lookout for the escape route.

If we follow God, we will never be put in a situation where we have to sin. However, if we are not following God, we will not have the strength or motivation to resist temptation.

As always, Jesus provides the perfect example for us to follow. When He was tempted in the wilderness, he resisted by quoting scripture. What He demonstrated was a simple, yet not always easy, reliance on what we know to be true.

When it comes to our relationship with God and every moral issue we will ever face, Jesus is the key. So let us go back to the basics for a moment. We know that God's word is true (John 17:17), we know that Jesus is truth (John 14:6), and we know that Jesus is the Word (John 1:1). Jesus said, "If you abide in My word, you are My disciples indeed. And you shall know the truth, and the truth shall make you free" (John 8:31-32), and "If the Son makes you free, you shall be free indeed" (John 8:36).

We may not always *feel* loved, but the Bible states clearly that we are (John 3:16). Therefore we can take comfort in that truth. Likewise, when we feel like sin has us in a chokehold, we can remember that God is gracious. We can take strength in knowing that God will provide a way out. We just need to look to Him. He will not lead us into temptation, but will deliver us from evil. He will do this to grow His kingdom, through His power, for His glory (Matthew 6:13).

Yes, temptations will come, but we know that God is faithful. He has called us to abide in Him, to be holy, and to live for His righteousness. God makes this possible by not allowing us to be tempted beyond what we can handle and by providing escape routes so that we can avoid sinning against Him.

On our own, we could never live up to God's standard of purity. But we overcome through faith in Jesus. It is in Him that we have the victory over sin. In His grace, He is ever-present to protect us against the power of temptation. And when we fail, He has made provision for us to be forgiven through the blood that He shed on the cross.

Please do not get numb to all this religious terminology. Do not miss the truth behind the words. Please understand that real victory over sin is not attained by saying more prayers or going to more church services. The core of everything is about having a healthy and personal relationship with Jesus. When we connect with Him, His presence changes everything!

Ultimately, whether we are relying on God to help us avoid temptation or we are calling out to Him after we fail, we are placing our faith whole-heartedly in Jesus, for He *is* our Great Escape.

Digging Deeper: James 1:12-16. Genesis 4:6-7. 2 Samuel 11:3. 1 Kings 11:1-13. 1 John 2: 1-2.

My Prayer to my Father:

_____

_____

_____

_____

_____

I will share what I learned with: _____

# Day 15

## The Fairness of God

*For we must all appear before the judgment seat of Christ, that each one may receive the things done in the body, according to what he has done, whether good or bad.*

- 2 Corinthians 5:10

As professing followers of Jesus Christ, we strive to do what is right in the sight of God. We endeavor to please Him here and now, even as we will throughout eternity, for we know that God is just.

I am not referring to salvation here, for that is determined by our faith in Jesus. When we believe in Jesus - that He is the Christ, the Son of God, and that His blood cleanses us of all our sins - we have eternal life.

In a sense, salvation is grace triumphing over judgment. God is able to keep His justice intact because the penalty for sin is paid in full by His

Son. We certainly do not deserve it, but God certainly thinks we are worth it!

That said, we will receive from God according to those things that we do now. Regardless of how things seem in the present time, there will come a day when everyone everywhere will stand before Christ and be judged. They will receive good from the Lord according to the good that they have done; and they will receive bad according to the bad that they have done.

Everyone has a sense for what is fair and what is unfair. Children are particularly keen to this concept. They will let you know right away when they think something is unfair. But though things do not always seem fair now, everyone will experience, first-hand, the fairness of God.

It is important to understand that the fairness of God is *not* our current quantity of money, talent, or IQ. His fairness is the consistent standard of morality that God will hold every one of us to. We are all equal under God's Law, and His judgments are based on His character, which never changes. He looks at our character, and what we have done with what we have been given.

Do not think that you will be judged against the standards of Adolf Hitler or Charles Manson, and thereby appear okay or even good when you stand before God. Neither should you worry about being compared to Mother Theresa or Billy Graham, and thus fall short of earning acceptance with God. But every one of us will be compared to that standard which was set by God, which is Christ Jesus our Lord.

Each person's calling is different, and each of us is responsible to perform all the things God has called us to do. Some of us were given more "talents" than others, some of us were hired late in the day, some of us have squandered literally everything like a prodigal son, but regardless, at the moment we put our faith in Jesus we are all called to be pure and live righteously.

Remember that we are talking about God's perspective when it comes to "good" and "bad." Being nice does not make you good in God's eyes. It will make relationships easier, but even atheists can be nice people.

All things done out of a love for God will count as "good". In the same way, all things done out of a love for self will count as "bad". On that day, it will be made known among all creation who we have served as supreme.

Let us then love God whole-heartedly with everything we set our mind on and what we think about. Let us love God with our soul and our passions. Let us love Him with all our strength and everything we set our hands to do. Let us do good by serving Him. Let us glorify Him by living for Him. For we know that nothing is hidden from the eyes of God - and we know that His judgments are perfect.

Digging Deeper:    Matthew 6:19-21.   1 Samuel 16:7. Revelation 20:11-15.

My Prayer to my Father:

_____

_____

_____

_____

_____

I will share what I learned with: _____

# Day 16

## On God's Team

*And it came to pass, when Joshua was by Jericho, that he lifted his eyes and looked, and behold, a Man stood opposite him with His sword drawn in his hand. And Joshua went to Him and said to Him, "Are You for us or for our adversaries?" So He said, "No, but as Commander of the army of the LORD I have now come." And Joshua fell on his face to the earth and worshiped, and said to Him, "What does my Lord say to His servant?"*

- Joshua 5:13-14

It is true - people like to pick sides. Whether it is a sports team, a political party, or even a church, we like to think that ours is the best.

Although almost all wars are motivated purely by politics and power, people on either side of the line like to believe that their cause is right and that God is with them. If anyone could have claimed that God was on their side, it would have been Joshua – as he was leading *God's* people into the land that *God* had promised to give them.

It is precisely this situation that makes the response of the "Man" so noteworthy. When Joshua asked Him if he was for them or for their enemies, He said "No."

Apparently, He was not content with the two options he was given. This Commander wanted to make it understood that He was on God's side, and that His allegiance was to God alone.

We ought to be fighting for righteous causes, both socially and morally, but we must resist the temptation to be consumed by our cause. We must not get so caught up in the struggle that we forget the One to whom we owe our highest allegiance.

Many wonderful ministries and effective missions have been birthed out of local churches. Yet, too many people are caught up in the church's culture and have forgotten about the church's purpose. They get focused on maintaining church business and programs and neglect the people outside their building. Other churches then become competition rather than partners in the kingdom of God. When they think their church is the only one that has it right, they set it up on a pedestal. They give their church a level of loyalty that should be reserved for God alone. Eventually, they can get so focused on themselves they forget to be a light to the community around them.

When our loyalty to our church, ministry, or cause takes priority over our loyalty to God, we have dethroned Him in our hearts. At this point, we have entered into idolatry. Remember, God is more interested in our purity than He is in our busyness. He does not want us to act religious, He wants us to take up our cross and humbly walk with Him.

We must not ignore Jesus; it is Him we represent. It is Him that we are living and working for from day to day. When our ministries, causes, and jobs are bathed in prayer and performed for God's glory, we are drawn closer to Him. This is when our hearts are purified, and His name is exalted.

As we build our lives and ministries, we must not displace the Cornerstone from our foundation. Our activities may seem good, but we must never let them distract us from our intimacy with Him. Nothing is to be more important to us than God, and God alone.

We can pray like King David, "Search me, O God, and know my heart; Try me, and know my anxieties; And see if there is any wicked way in me, And lead me in the way everlasting" (Psalm 139:23-24). Let us put aside every sin and every attitude that grieves His Holy Spirit. Let us settle in our hearts that Jesus is Lord and that He is our only

King. Let us decide today that no matter what happens in life, we will be on God's side and that our highest loyalty will be to Him alone.

Digging Deeper:    Exodus 20:2-3.   Joshua 24:15. Luke 14:25-33.

My Prayer to my Father:

_____

_____

_____

_____

_____

I will share what I learned with: _____

# Day 17

## Just One Last Step

*So the scribe said to Him, "Well said, Teacher. You have spoken the truth, for there is one God, and there is no other but He. And to love Him with all the heart, with all the understanding, with all the soul, and with all the strength, and to love one's neighbor as oneself, is more than all the whole burnt offerings and sacrifices." Now when Jesus saw that he answered wisely, He said to him, "You are not far from the kingdom of God." But after that no one dared question Him.*

- Mark 12:32-34

When Jesus was asked which commandment was the first, or most important, commandment of all, He responded with His famous quotation of Deuteronomy 6:4-5 and Leviticus 19:18, saying that we are to love the one, true God with all of our heart, soul, mind and strength, and that we are to love our neighbor as ourselves.

Jesus made it clear that *love* was God's highest

requirement for mankind. God Himself was to be the object of our highest affection. Additionally, the well-being of others was to be our second priority.

Unlike many of his peers, the scribe that had asked this question seemed genuinely interested in Jesus's response. He was one of the few religious leaders who recognized and attested to the truthfulness of Jesus's words. He was, in fact, closer than most in comprehending the nature of God and His purpose for our lives. He understood that such love was far more important in the eyes of God than mere burnt offerings and sacrifices. When his response reflected this conviction, Jesus proclaimed, "You are not far from the kingdom of God."

A clear understanding of what God desires is a fundamental part of a Christian's life. To understand that God loves you and everyone around you is a great starting point. To recognize that we need to love God back and care for others is to be very close to being a part of the kingdom of God.

In Mark 10:17-22, we see a rich young man who was also only one step away from being in the kingdom of heaven. He claimed he had kept God's laws since he was a child, but wanted to know what else he needed to do to have eternal life. Jesus offered him everything he wanted and more. Jesus offered him the opportunity to follow Him. At the same time, He exposed what the man desired more than eternal life: wealth.

Although we do not know the outcome of the previous scribe's encounter with Jesus, we know that this rich ruler was not willing to give up everything he had in order to follow Jesus.

Sadly, there are many people today who recognize Jesus as a good man or even a prophet, but they stop short of recognizing Him as the Messiah and King of kings. They want to be spiritual, they want others to think that they are a good person, but they are not willing to humble themselves before God and completely surrender their life to Jesus.

To partake of God's kingdom, we must put our faith in Jesus and set Him up as Lord in our heart. This is an all-encompassing decision, which will affect every part of our life. He alone is to have our highest affection and absolute loyalty.

We must surrender everything and follow Him. Only then can we walk in the light of God's love. Only then will we be able to truly love God and others as He intended.

May we seek to return the adoration that He has shown toward us by loving Him with all our heart, mind, soul, and strength. And may we reflect His compassion on those around us by loving them like He has loved us.

Digging Deeper:   John 6:47-69 & 12:24-26 & 15:12-13.


My Prayer to my Father:

_____

_____

_____

_____

_____

I will share what I learned with: _____

# Day 18

## "Jesus Saves"

*And she will bring forth a Son, and you shall call His name JESUS, for He will save His people from their sins.*

- Matthew 1:21

Joseph was instructed by an angel in a dream to name Mary's first son "Jesus". The name in Hebrew, Yeshua, actually means *Yahweh is Salvation*. The angel of the Lord even stated exactly what Jesus would be saving people from. This was an early indication of Jesus's deity, since only God can save people from their sins.

When Jesus was born, an angel appeared to some nearby shepherds and proclaimed, "For there is born to you this day in the city of David a Savior, who is Christ the Lord" (Luke 2:11). The Greek word for "savior" can be defined as deliverer, preserver, healer, and protector. The Greek word for "Christ" is equivalent to the Hebrew word for "Messiah", both of which mean "Anointed One."

This is amazingly good news! We have all made mistakes; we have all offended God. Our sins have literally divided and separated us from God. The word *sin* can also mean that we have "missed the mark" (an archery term in reference to missing the bull's eye). To miss the mark implies that we were trying to hit something in the first place.

Much of the world into which Jesus was born made two crucial mistakes: They were not aiming for the right target, and they did not recognize their Savior!

Most of the Jews were so caught up in the politics of the day that they lost sight of what they really needed to be saved from. They thought they needed to be delivered from the Roman Empire, but God knew that their real need was to be delivered from their sins. Their political situation was horrible, but it was not as important as their relationship to God. The Roman government was not standing between them and their God - their sins were!

Today, our need is the same. We do not need to be delivered from poverty, our parents, uncool clothes, a political party, or even the pains of life itself. These are just distractions and external problems. Our real need is much deeper. What we desperately need is to be saved from our sins.

From God's perspective, the most important thing we need is a pure relationship with Him. This relationship should be at the top of our priority list as well. Sin is the one thing that stands in the way of this closeness, and should, therefore, be abhorred as the enemy that it is.

We need to repent. But that word is often misused and misunderstood in our culture. Sadly, the self-righteous indignation of prideful preachers has tainted its true meaning. To repent is to turn away from something. It is a 180-degree change of direction. It is to change our perspective so that it lines up with God's perspective. It is to stop going where we want and start going where God wants.

There can be no forgiveness without repentance. If we are not willing to turn away from our sin, how can God forgive that sin? Repentance is the golden gate we walk through as we fall into the loving arms of a merciful God.

Jesus shed His blood and died on the cross to make atonement for our sins and then rose from the dead three days later. He paid the penalty for our sin and took on Himself the punishment we deserved. He did this so that we would have the supernatural power to do what is right in God's eyes. He did this so we could live together with Him forever.

Let us therefore rejoice in God's grace – the gift of

a Savior, the deliverance from our sins, and the ability to hit the bull's eye!

Digging Deeper:    Luke 5:18-26 & 7:48-50.    John 8:3-11.

My Prayer to my Father:

_____

_____

_____

_____

_____

I will share what I learned with: _____

# Day 19

## Thinking Holy Spirit Thoughts

*For those who live according to the flesh set their minds on the things of the flesh, but those who live according to the Spirit, the things of the Spirit.*

*So then, those who are in the flesh cannot please God.*

- Romans 8:5, 8

It is a sobering thought…that our lifestyle can actually render us incapable of pleasing God. As followers of Christ, pleasing God should be our heart's highest desire. As humans created in His image, glorifying God is actually our main purpose for existing (Isaiah 43:7). It is something we should live for and something we should think about.

Sometimes it is easy for us to point a finger at the socially rebellious and those who live self-destructive lives, and accuse them of being "in the flesh." Unfortunately, many people who seem very religious also fall into this description and are equally displeasing to God.

The "spiritual leaders" of Jesus's day were the focus of His harshest rebukes. Being carnal and not spiritual can derail us just as easily today. No one is immune. Pastors and church leaders must be just as careful as the people who sit in the pews every Sunday.

We must guard against a very dangerous spiritual hypocrisy if we are to love God with all of our heart, mind, soul, and strength. Too many people live according to their flesh but like to think that they are spiritual. By their own efforts, they are diligent to live a clean life, but in reality they harbor a carnal mind. They are depending on what they can do instead of what Jesus has done.

Righteousness is obtained only by faith in Jesus Christ. It cannot be acquired by keeping laws and rules. Adhering to rules and upholding traditions may make us look good on the outside, but they do not make us pure on the inside. These outward works do not necessarily increase our intimacy with God, nor do they always cause us to grow in our love for Him (Romans 8:1- 2).

We must also guard against compromises and self-justifications. Sometimes we allow sin to creep in and pretend that it is not that bad because we are still doing some good stuff. We could get drunk on a Saturday then tell ourselves we are not that bad because we went to church on Sunday. Perhaps we look at porn and justify it in our mind because we are not physically cheating on our spouse. Maybe we compromise our calling to forgive others by harboring just a little bitterness toward someone who has hurt us. The bottom line is this; any compromise grieves the heart of God and hurts the people around us.

Again, if we are overly focused on keeping the rules of a church or a pet doctrine, we tend to do so by our own efforts. Thus we are minding the flesh and are not living in the Spirit. Our flesh-trap is complete when we deceive ourselves into thinking that it is the keeping of these man-made rules or side doctrines that make us right with God.

We are not made righteous by keeping the law in our flesh, but by turning our hearts toward God and putting our faith in His Son (Romans 8:3). When we do this, we are living according to the Spirit. When we are living according to the Spirit, we set our minds on the things of the Spirit. When we set our minds on the things of the Spirit, we please God.

The Holy Spirit leads us in seemingly random ways at times. He is unpredictable like the wind. We often do not know where He is going or what He is going to do next. Our job is to follow; His promise is to provide.

Like Paul, let us put no confidence in our flesh (Philippians 3:3). Our status and titles do not impress God; our love does. Our works do not make us holy; our faith in Jesus does. Let us bring glory and pleasure to God by listening to and obeying the Holy Spirit. Let us represent His kingdom to the world by bringing our hearts, our thoughts, and our lifestyles into alignment with His Spirit.

Digging Deeper: Matthew 6:33. John 3:1-12.
1 Corinthians 3:1-3 & 10:31.

My Prayer to my Father:

_____

_____

_____

_____

_____

I will share what I learned with: _____

# Day 20

## Good Guidance

*Then the men of Israel took some of their provisions; but they did not ask counsel of the LORD.*

- Joshua 9:14

After 400 years in Egypt, the children of Israel began to enter the land that God had promised to their father, Abraham. As instructed by the Lord, they began to destroy or drive out the civilizations that were there. While most of the inhabitants prepared for battle, a group of Gibeonites decided to try a different plan. They put on old clothes, packed dry, moldy bread into well-worn sacks, and set out to deceive the Israelites.

Their plan worked only because the leaders of Israel made one vital mistake. They listened to their story and took note of their appearance, but they neglected to inquire of God before entering into a covenant with the travelers.

This created a massive dilemma. They had been told by God to conquer the people of the land, but they had sworn an oath to these men by the Lord God of Israel. Because they did not seek God's guidance, there was anger and confusion among the people of God (Joshua 9:18).

Today, God desires that we also enter into His rest, the place He has prepared for us. Like the Israelites, God goes before us and becomes the method and power by which we repent of our sins and die to our selfishness. He has clearly outlined in His Word how we are to walk before Him in purity, but there are many day-to-day decisions that He leaves up to us. Even in these, He desires that we seek Him first. Do we consult Him in prayer before we buy a car or house? Do we seek His guidance when we look for a new job, or when we look for new ways to share God's love with a neighbor? Is religion something we do on Sunday mornings, or is Jesus someone we follow and obey on a daily basis?

As God led His people out of Egypt, He instructed them along the way. Today, Jesus instructs us to follow Him. Part of following Him means keeping our eyes focused on Him, and not on the things around us. Peter was able to walk on water *only* when he kept his eyes on Jesus and believed. When he focused on the large waves around him, he began to sink. Unfortunately, it is very easy for us to get tripped up and distracted by outward appearances.

Although God may not always give us a clear answer to our questions, He is faithful to direct us where He wants us to go. He has a purpose for us to fulfill, and we have an important part to play within the body of Christ. Because He desires an intimate relationship with us, He wants us to be active and involved in this process.

When we seek God for guidance, we are, in essence, making Him our priority. To God, this reflects a heart of submission and a willingness to obey. This simple act of submission can, and should be, the natural reaction of those who desire to please Him and do His will. In fact, this diligent search for God's will and purpose in our lives can reveal so much more: a heart that loves Him.

This, of course, is the pinnacle and essence of the Christian faith: that we allow God to develop in us a heart that loves Him completely and unreservedly. Let us be diligent therefore, not to let the things around us distract or deceive us. Let us earnestly seek God and His council as we follow Him every day.

Digging Deeper:  Exodus 34:10-17.  2 Samuel 21:1-14.  Matthew 7:7-11.


My Prayer to my Father:

_____

_____

_____

_____

_____


I will share what I learned with: _____

# Day 21

## Divorce According to Jesus

*They said, "Moses permitted a man to write a certificate of divorce, and to dismiss her." And Jesus answered and said to them, "Because of the hardness of your heart he wrote you this precept. But from the beginning of the creation, God 'made them male and female.' For this reason a man shall leave his father and mother and be joined to his wife, 'and the two shall become one flesh'; so then they are no longer two, but one flesh. Therefore what God has joined together, let not man separate.*

- Mark 10:4-9

The Pharisees once again tried to trap Jesus in His words. This time they brought up the issue of divorce - obviously a touchy subject even 2,000 years ago. They knew that Moses had permitted it

(Deuteronomy 24). They also knew that the prophet Malachi had said that God hates divorce (Malachi 2:13-16). If Jesus were to defend one of these prophets, they would be able to accuse Him of defying the other.

To support and defend this special relationship, Jesus chooses to refer them back to the beginning. He spells out God's original design for marriage by describing how a man is to leave his parents and join with his wife, thus creating an all-new family unit (Genesis 2:24). The physical, emotional, and spiritual bond is so great that they are now perceived as "one flesh".

God created Adam and Eve in His own image, and then proclaimed his new creation to be "very good" (Genesis 1:31). From that time until now, the marriage relationship has maintained a unique and vital role in His eyes.

The marriage union is so dynamic that it is even used to illustrate our relationship with Jesus! He tells a parable in Matthew 25:1-13 that likens us to virgins waiting for the bridegroom. Upon hearing of Jesus' growing number of disciples, John the Baptist proclaimed, "He who has the bride is the bridegroom" (John 3:29). In Revelation 19:7-9, we get a glimpse of the marriage of the Lamb to His wife dressed in white linen – which represents the saints, who are clothed in righteousness.

A marriage, therefore, is much more than just a

piece of paper. It is to be a *covenant* between a man and a woman before God. It is a solemn vow to love and honor the other no matter what. Strong feelings may bring them together, but it is their commitment to each other and the grace of God that will make the marriage last through the years. God created marriage to be unique among human relationships, and God intended it be permanent. As Christians, we should have this same perspective.

Today, as in Jesus' day, some have fallen short of God's ideal. Divorce among those who claim to be Christians is alarmingly high. We seem to have adopted the world's mindset rather than Christ's.

As at other times when we fail and fall short, there is grace and forgiveness. We can always come back to Christ. And there is no condemnation to those who are in Christ. It is never too late to bring our thoughts and views into agreement with God's perspective on the topic, and to do everything in our power to bring our life and choices in line with God's will.

God still hates divorce. It still runs contrary to His nature. The sad fact is divorce does great damage to everyone involved, including the kids. Divorce tears relationships apart, but God's heart is to reconcile and restore relationships through love.

Sometimes life gets messy, though, and people make mistakes. Yes, there are times when God still allows divorce (like in the case of an unbeliever who wants to leave, or when adultery has occurred). But even then, God is still God, and He still holds us in His hands. His love for us never falters or fails, even if human love grows cold or betrays us.

Jesus was blunt when He pointed out that a hard heart is the root cause of divorce. Let us, therefore, be diligent to maintain a soft heart toward God and our spouse. Let us practice patience and kindness. When we are struggling with a spouse, we need to be diligent to maintain an attitude of forgiveness. Let us put away the poison of bitterness. Let us put on humility so that we can honestly face our faults and put our spouse first.

Most importantly, we need to commit our most important relationship to God. What Jesus has spoken, let us hold up as truth; and what God has joined together, let no man tear apart.

Digging Deeper:    Matthew 19:3-12.    1 Peter 3:1-7. Ephesians 5:1-33.    Colossians 3:18-19.

My Prayer to my Father:

_____

_____

_____

_____

_____

I will share what I learned with: _____

# Day 22

## Living Faith

*Behold the proud, his soul is not upright in him;*
*But the just shall live by his faith.*

- Habakkuk 2:4

Faith, in its most common Biblical sense, means simply "trust" or "reliance". Even before Jesus came, faith was not merely obeying the law. Faith was and is a confidence in the faithfulness of God to keep His word. True faith results in a loving obedience to God's will at all times.

Throughout the Old Testament we see numerous examples of men and women who trusted in God, and who lived by faith. Many of these are listed in Hebrews 11; people like Abel, Enoch, Noah, Abraham, Sarah, and Moses.

The New Testament repeatedly encourages us to have faith in Jesus and His atoning sacrifice. It requires faith to believe that Jesus was the Messiah, the Son of the Living God. It requires faith to believe that the blood Jesus shed on the cross is sufficient to cleanse us of all sin, guilt, and shame.

If we believe in God and follow Him, He justifies us by His Son. Jesus made it clear that faith in Him was absolutely necessary for eternal life.

While reading the Bible increases our knowledge about God, faith that is acceptable to God must go beyond a simple knowledge of what the Bible says. Many people claim to "believe" that Jesus is the Christ, but they have not made Him the Lord and Master of their life. To admit that there is a God is one thing, to submit to Him, commit yourself to follow Him, and actually love Him with all your heart is quite another.

True faith in Jesus will always and inevitably produce a holy life. It is putting into action our beliefs concerning God. James says that faith without works is dead (James 2:20). This does **not** mean we have to work for our salvation. It means that if we do not live out what we say we believe, then we do not really believe it. For better or worse, our lives are a reflection of what we really believe in our heart.

John clarifies further when he explains that if we say we love God but do not love people, we are lying (1 John 4:20). If we love a God who's nature is love, how can we possibly be unloving?

Many people have heard the term "saving faith". It should be pointed out that the faith that saves is the same faith that keeps! The same faith that grafts us, like a branch, into the vine also gives us the ability to bear spiritual fruit (Galatians 5:22-23). Faith does not just kick start our Christian life, it defines it every day.

Anything other than a life lived by faith in God is a reflection of pride. If a person is arrogant, their soul is not upright. If we reject God and refuse to follow Jesus, it is because we have placed ourselves above our Creator and our desires take priority over His. That is pride.

Proud people have a serious problem. Because they do not believe in Jesus, they are condemned already. They are under God's condemnation because when the light of the world makes Himself known to them, they choose to stay in darkness. They love their sin more than God.

As our main verse implies, pride corrupts the soul. It will also cause God to actively resist us (James 4:6; 1 Peter 5:5). While true faith is focused only on the reliability of God, pride is a focus and reliance on ourselves. Even so, God's grace always leaves room for redemption. The Holy Spirit can always convict us of our sin and draw us back to Christ.

To actively love, it must be focused on someone. There must be an object of our affection. I can say I love my son because he is the object of my affection and the focus of my adoration.

In the same way, faith must have a focus. And God must be the object of our faith. Just like love, true faith only functions within the context of an intimate relationship with God.

Our relationship with Him must affect every aspect of our life. When He reveals Himself to us in a genuine encounter, we change! The opposite is also true. If He reaches out to us and we reject Him, we change then too, but not in a good way.

So why do we need faith? Because without faith, it is impossible to please God (Hebrews 11:6). How do we get faith? Faith comes by hearing, and hearing by the Word of God (Romans 10:17). The Bible is the Word of God, and God is not a man that He should lie (Numbers 23:19). We, then, should be fully persuaded that what God has promised, He is able to perform (Romans 4:21). Therefore, my friends, have faith in God (Mark 11:22).

Digging Deeper:   John 3:18-19 & 14:6-7 & 15:1-8.

My Prayer to my Father:

_____

_____

_____

_____

_____

I will share what I learned with: _____

# Day 23

## The War Between
## Love and Lust

*You have heard that it was said to those of old,
'You shall not commit adultery.' But I say to you
that whoever looks at a woman to lust for her has
already committed adultery with her in his heart.*

- Matthew 5:27-28

God made a man. And seeing that this man was
alone and without a sufficient companion, God, in
His wisdom and goodness, created a woman. A
man's attraction to a woman is natural and God-
given, but like anything else, it can be degraded and
perverted. Attraction descends into lust when it
becomes self-centered and self-serving.

To love a woman is to give her the emotional
support and attention she needs, and to encourage
her to walk closer with God. By contrast, lust is

when my gratification is more important than her purity. To lust after a woman is to desire her to please me more than I desire her to please God.

Was Jesus serious when he made the statement in this verse? Did he know what he was talking about? Is this really God's perspective on adultery? The answer to these questions should be an unquestionable "Yes!" To look at a woman in such a manner is just as displeasing to God as literally breaking the law "You shall not commit adultery" (Ex. 20:14).

If a man is a true follower of God, he cannot continue to live in disobedience to His law. If someone loves God with all their heart, they will not continue to do the things that He hates. James describes clearly where such a path will lead. To continue in this or any other sin will eventually lead to death and separation from God (James 1:14-15).

Jesus spoke the truth that day when he expounded on adultery and lust. He also gave a keen insight as to how God the Father esteems inner purity. God requires His people not only to control their actions, but also their mind, their eyes, and their motives. What is at stake here is the condition of our heart. It is an issue of character. It is an issue of purity. And God is chiefly concerned with these things!

Some may argue that such fantasies do no harm. The truth is the damage is initially internal. But an unclean heart will eventually expose itself in outward actions, and if these sins are not dealt with correctly, they will cause us to hurt others, and ultimately they will lead to eternal death.

To allow our selves to give in to lust is to set our heart against God. We cannot say, "Your kingdom come" when we are actively seeking to entice women away from purity, holiness, and godliness. We cannot promote the freedom of the Gospel while simultaneously supporting an industry that degrades and dehumanizes women. God's love and our lust are at war with each other.

We cannot love in word and deed while at the same time lusting in our heart and mind. What goes on inside of us will eventually come out. If we do not sow the seeds of lust, we will not reap the harvest of adultery. We should be able to say with Job, "I made a covenant with my eyes not to look lustfully at a young woman" (Job 31:1 [NIV]).

God's desire is that we love one another. To lust after a woman is to, in our minds, degrade them from being a human, created in God's image, to being merely a toy or inanimate object to be used for our own pleasure. To love them is to see them in the light of what Jesus did for them. His death on the cross for that woman's salvation is the true indicator of her value and how precious she is to Him.

When Jesus encountered vulnerable women, He

offered them honor, respect, and eternal life. He is calling us to do the same.

So how do we get there? First, we ask God to forgive us for our lust. We spend time with God and submit to His will. We commit to loving people like Jesus does. We pray for our own heart to be pure. Second, we pray for the women. We intercede for them and ask that God would keep them pure, show them their true value, and protect them from those who would take advantage of them.

While this chapter is focused mainly on men, many women also desire to be with people they should not be with. For some, it may be more emotional than physical. Women generally long for security, affection, comfort, and protection. But if they are looking for those things in someone other than their spouse, they are in the same boat.

Both women and men need to learn to be content with God's provision. He wants us to understand that we are complete in God's love.

Remember, we are not alone in this battle. God's Holy Spirit is with us and in us. He is in our corner; He is on our side. And He has more than enough power to set us free.

Digging Deeper:    Proverbs 6:20-35 & 7:1-27.
Romans 13:13-14.   1 Thessalonians 4:3-8.   Galatians
5:16-26.


My Prayer to my Father:

_____

_____

_____

_____

_____


I will share what I learned with: _____

# Day 24

## "God Bless America"

*To you first, God, having raised up His Servant Jesus, sent Him to bless you, in turning away every one of you from your iniquities.*

- Acts 3:26

Here in America, we have become accustomed to hearing politicians end their speeches with a resolute, "God bless America." In our churches, it is very common to hear someone say, "I am blessed" or "God bless you." These phrases sound good, but what are we really trying to communicate?

Here, in the book of Acts, Peter had just gone up to the temple with John to pray. As they went, they met a man who was crippled and could not walk. Peter looked at him and said, "In the name of Jesus Christ of Nazareth rise up and walk" (vs. 6).

And he did.

Being healed, the man went with them into the temple, walking, and leaping, and praising God. When the people recognized him as the one who begged outside the gate, they ran to see what had happened and were amazed. Presented with an attentive audience, Peter preaches repentance from sin and faith in Jesus Christ, whom God had raised from the dead. He then ended with our main quote above.

It is important to note the context of the blessing. "To you first" refers to the Jewish people. This same blessing was then offered to everyone - as many as would believe. Peter tells them that Jesus is the fulfillment of God's promise to Abraham, that "in your seed all the families of the earth shall be blessed" (vs. 25).

The exact nature of the blessing now comes into focus. Although a supernatural healing had just taken place, these kinds of things were not the blessings that would fulfill the ancient promise. It showed the power of Christ and bore witness to the resurrection, but it was not the Abrahamic blessing that was to go unto every nation.

Jesus Christ is the "seed" of Abraham that blesses the world. The essence of this blessing is that we are turned from our iniquities in order to serve the true and living God.

The Greek word for bless, *yoo-log-eh'-o*, means

to speak well of (like a eulogy at a funeral). It is made up of two root words: *yoo* (good) and *logos* (word). God wants to speak a "good word" over us. He wants to speak life to our souls.

This word can also mean "thank, prosper, and praise." Yes, God wants to "prosper" us, but not necessarily with money. Sadly, too many Americans only seem to think of blessings in financial terms. Fortunately for all of us, God's intended blessings are much more holistic. In turning us from our iniquities, He benefits us spiritually, socially, mentally, emotionally, and physically.

He may not double our bank account, but He will meet our needs. He may not protect us from all trouble, but He will give us peace in the hard times. He may not give us abundant pleasure now, but He will give us abundant life. But this life can only be found in Him. As always, God is far more concerned with who we are than what we have.

He not only wants us to stop doing those things that He hates, He wants us to be more like Him. And God is love. He is also holy and righteous. For our good and for His glory, He wants to bless us by turning us from our sins.

Let us receive God's blessing with joy! Let us turn away from the behaviors that grieve His Spirit and break His heart. If we want God to bless America, we must let Him start with us!

Being set free from sin, we can now live righteously. We can now love without fear. We can now seek to establish His kingdom and not our own.

Having been blessed by God by having our sin washed away by the blood of Jesus, we can now bless God by thanking Him, by praising Him, and by speaking well of Him.

Digging Deeper:   Mark 1:14-15.   Ezekiel 33:11. Ephesians 4:29-30.

My Prayer to my Father:

_____

_____

_____

_____

_____

I will share what I learned with: _____

# Day 25

## To Rejoice or not to Rejoice

*My brethren, count it all joy when you fall into various trials, knowing that the testing of your faith produces patience. But let patience have its perfect work, that you may be perfect and complete, lacking nothing.*

- James 1:2-4

*Nevertheless do not rejoice in this, that the spirits are subject to you, but rather rejoice because your names are written in heaven.*

- Luke 10:20

Are you like me? Do you have a tendency to rejoice at the wrong time, over the wrong thing? Many times, God's principles seem odd at first. They are contrary to the selfishness with which we are accustomed. As Christians we are to love those that hate us; we are to forgive those that wrong us; we are to bless those that curse us; and according to the book of James, we are to rejoice when we struggle with temptations.

Obviously, God operates on a different set of principles, and has a different objective than we do.

At first, all we can see is the difficulty and inconvenience of the moment. God wants to take us above that and show us the humility, maturity, and benevolence that will result from such struggles. Much of how we grow in life depends on our attitude and if we choose to see things how God sees them. Instead of concentrating on the severity of our circumstances we are to look forward to the perfecting of our faith.

The Greek word for "patience" can also mean "endurance". In other words, we are to develop, in our characters, a trait of "patient continuance". Unfortunately, it seems this is developed mainly as we struggle through various trials and temptations. However, when our patience is perfected, we will be perfect, wanting nothing.

Years ago, someone in church light-heartedly warned me, "Don't ever pray for patience, because God will test you." I understand his sentiment. I know how grueling it can be to have my patience tested. But something about his words grieved me. I wondered if he truly understood the massive spiritual benefit that such tests can bring.

We do not usually need to ask for such things

anyway. It does not take much for God to show us how weak we really are, and Satan is constantly tempting us or knocking us down.

Trials and temptations will always come. Instead of inviting them or seeking them out, we should prepare our heart and stay grounded in God's Word. Then we will be able stand firm in our faith in Christ when they hit us like a flood.

It is this standing in Christ, this trusting God through the trial, this faithfulness, that is a mark of our spiritual maturity. We should rejoice in *everything* that draws us closer to our Heavenly Father, regardless of how unpleasant.

There is a flip side to this equation: How do we react when things go really well? God has blessed us with many things. Most notably, He has blessed us with the Holy Spirit, and the power to do everything He desires us to do. Perhaps God has recently helped us resist a temptation, or He may have just answered a desperate prayer. At times, He may even desire to work a miracle through us in order to accomplish His purpose and bring about His kingdom. He may actually lead us to cast a demon out of someone. But even these times of triumph should not be our source of real joy. Rather, our joy and confidence should rest on His acceptance of us through Jesus Christ.

We are not to rejoice in a lack of trials, nor are we to rejoice in the healing, delivering power that

Jesus gives to his servants. We are to rejoice in our development of patient endurance, which leads to perfect faith. We are to rejoice in the fact that our names are written in heaven. We are to rejoice in our God, not in our circumstances. We are to rejoice in the Lord always. So rejoice!

Digging Deeper:   Philippians 4:4.  Psalm 118:21-29. John 15:11-13.  1 John 1:1-4.

My Prayer to my Father:

_____
_____
_____
_____
_____

I will share what I learned with: _____

# Day 26

## It is an Abomination

*Likewise also the men, leaving the natural use of the woman, burned in their lust for one another, men with men committing what is shameful, and receiving in themselves the penalty of their error which was due. And even as they did not like to retain God in their knowledge, God gave them over to a debased mind, to do those things which are not fitting.*

- Romans 1:27-28

For Christians, the debate over homosexuality is not just a political hot-button issue. As people who love God, follow Jesus, and believe in the Bible, it is first and foremost a *moral* issue.

The things that are important to God, He has communicated in plain and simple language through His Word. If this topic was never mentioned in

Scripture, then we could debate over whether it was good or bad. But this is not the case. God's view of this behavior has been clearly and consistently expressed throughout both the Old and New Testaments.

The first mention of this particular activity is found in the story of Sodom and Gomorrah (Genesis 19). It is one of the reasons God destroyed those cities. In Genesis 18:20, God said, "their sin is very grave." Their sin is mentioned in Ezekiel 16:49-50 as flowing out of their pride and arrogance. Both 2 Peter 2:6 and Jude 7 tell us that they were destroyed as an example to the ungodly.

In case there was any doubt about this story and the lessons to be learned, God settles the issue permanently when He says, "You shall not lie with a male, as with a woman. It is an abomination" (Leviticus 18:22). This sentiment is repeated again in Leviticus 20:13 and in Romans 1:24-32, which is partially quoted above. It is also important to note that 1 Corinthians 6:9-20 and Galatians 5:19-24 clearly includes this behavior in the lists of things that will keep us from inheriting the kingdom of God.

As Christians, we need to guard against hypocrisy. Too many religious people seem eager to condemn homosexuals, while they themselves practice one or more of the other behaviors listed in Corinthians and Galatians. Sin is sin, and heterosexual fornication and adultery are just as offensive to God. We all need to love God more than we love pleasure.

God designed relationships to function in a certain way. He wants us to care for and love our spouse, and together love and raise the children that come from that union. As a protective Father, His compassionate love for us forbids any behavior that would cause damage to ourselves or these core relationships.

We need to understand that advocates of homosexuality base their opinions on modern political and social concepts, rather than on the Word of God. They have not made the Bible their foundation for truth. An honest study of Scripture would never lead someone to believe that God approves of this behavior. God has never changed His stance on this issue. Nowhere in the Bible can we observe His attitude shift from *abomination* to *approval*.

This is a highly charged issue in our culture. We must clearly understand God's perspective and we must be prepared to address the issue in a Christ-like way. We must be willing to stand on His Word and submit our life to His will. As Christians, we need to seek to know the heart of God, for this is just one of the many issues facing us today. In all things, we need to love God enough to stay pure ourselves, and also stand up for what is right, good, and pure.

With that said, we must be careful to speak the truth *in love*. Our words must be grounded in humility and flow from genuine compassion. Jesus said that He did not come to condemn the world, and we were not put here to do that either! Love is what should be motivating us when we let others know that their immoral behavior will not only destroy them physically and emotionally, but will keep them from an intimate and enjoyable relationship with Jesus Christ.

When talking about such topics as this, may we be ever mindful of the grace that God has shown us in our own struggles and temptations. It is only through His power that we are set free, and it is only through His power that others will be set free. May we be motivated by love and compassion, and speak with humility and grace. And may we always be focused on the ultimate goal: a lost soul being reconciled to God.

Digging Deeper:   1 John 1:5-10.   John 3:17-19 & 8:3-12.

My Prayer to my Father:

_____

_____

_____

_____

_____

I will share what I learned with: _____

# Day 27

## Repentance + Faith

*Testifying to Jews, and also to Greeks, repentance toward God and faith toward our Lord Jesus Christ.*

- Acts 20:21

Paul is wrapping up a brief account of his behavior in Ephesus by explaining how he had ministered to both the Jews and the Greeks – preaching both repentance and faith.

Repeatedly, the Bible ties together the ideas of repentance from sin and faith in Jesus. Almost as a single unit, these two actions are intimately connected. Faith and repentance were never intended to function independently. One should not happen without the other.

If a person were to accept one part of this duo, while ignoring the other, it would result in either a

125

misguided repentance or a worthless faith. Either of these would be a sad state of existence, because both miss out on the fullness of God's grace. We cannot turn toward God if we do not believe in Jesus, and we cannot pretend to follow Jesus if we are still wallowing in our sin.

Scripture makes it clear that faithful living *must* accompany true repentance. To try to repent without a change of lifestyle would be an insincere and false repentance. When repentance is genuine, it leads to a restitution of wrongs and a deep commitment to wrong no more.

When faith is real, it too becomes an active part of our life. We are to live with our eyes fixed on Jesus. Our love for God and for other people will be the evidence of our faith. We will learn to trust God to meet our needs in both bad times and good. With faith, we will learn to hear and obey His voice.

Repentance becomes a consistent part of our life because we are constantly messing up and missing the target. God desires us to be pure, but we cannot be pure in God's eyes unless He cleanses us. And the only thing that can cleanse us is the blood of Jesus Christ. That is why trying to repent without faith is useless, our faith is in the Son of God and the forgiveness, redemption, and restoration He accomplished for us on the cross.

Our faith in Christ, however, is not limited to

those moments when we are seeking God's forgiveness. This is just a starting point! God desires us to live righteously. He wants us to live right in His eyes, to live for His glory, and to care about others. Essentially, He wants us to live and walk in His love.

The same Divine power and kindness that lifts us out of our darkness is the same power and kindness that sustains us and guides us as we live in His light. It is faith in Jesus that saves us from our sins, and it is this same faith in Jesus that makes our lives more holy every day.

So first, let us pursue His face in a quiet place. Let us put aside every rebellious act and false idea. Let us commit ourselves to following His lead. Let us strive to stand before God repentant and pure, and to walk before Him in faith and love.

Then, as we do this, may we step out in faith and encourage others to turn toward God. May we pray for them and share with them the good news of God's love and the freedom and eternal life He wants to give them through Jesus. May we encourage them to turn to God and put their faith in Jesus.

Digging Deeper:   Matthew 4:17.   Acts 19:18-20.
Luke 3:7-14.   John 11:21-27.

My Prayer to my Father:

_____

_____

_____

_____

_____

I will share what I learned with: _____

# Day 28

## Acceptance Without Tolence

*When Jesus had raised Himself up and saw no one but the woman, He said to her, "Woman, where are those accusers of yours? Has no one condemned you?" She said, "No one, Lord." And Jesus said to her, "Neither do I condemn you; go and sin no more."*

- John 8:10-11

To accept someone is to love them, regardless of their race, gender, religion, or crime. To tolerate someone is, according to Webster's Dictionary, to "allow deviation". Differences in personality and opinions must be given their space, for every individual has a different gift and calling from God. But while this freedom is granted, we must not allow the truth of God's Word to be compromised or disregarded.

We must love people relentlessly without deviating from God's truth. We must always accept people, but we are never to accept sin. To allow someone to continue in self-destructive behavior and not reach out to them would be to *not* love them. The same principle applies to spiritual things. To allow someone to continue in sinful behavior without warning them of the eternal consequences is the opposite of love.

Like Jesus, our ultimate goal is to reconcile people to God. If we truly understand that a person's sin will keep them out of God's presence, our love for them should compel us to address it. To refuse to address it is to *not* love them or want what is best for them.

As always, we must look to Jesus Christ, who exemplified this balance between acceptance and tolerance. Time after time, He was placed in situations where He had to juggle the Father's mercy and justice. The story of the woman caught in adultery is a classic example of how Jesus illustrated both holiness and compassion.

The Pharisees and other religious leaders were continually questioning Him, trying to trick Him into saying something that they could use against Him. This time it regarded the Law of Moses. They brought to Him a woman, guilty without question. Jesus knew it, she knew it, and the crowd knew it. All that remained was Jesus's response.

Had He condemned her to death, He could have been accused of defying Rome, because only the Romans had the authority to carry out capital punishment at that time. Had he let her go free, He could have been accused of disregarding the Law of Moses. Without disloyalty to either, He said, "He who is without sin among you, let him throw a stone at her first" (vs. 7). He took the focus off of her sin and put the spotlight on their sin.

He could have condemned her according to the law and upheld God's justice and righteousness. But He did not come to condemn, but to demonstrate God's mercy. If He had said to stone her to death, we would be tempted to become "trigger happy" – poised to crush anyone not living up to *our* standard, just like the Pharisees. Instead, we ought to humbly remember that we were also sinners who needed mercy.

Although Jesus chose to show compassion, He did not excuse or tolerate her sin. He did not allow her to deviate from the law or condone her behavior when He refused to condemn her to death. Rather, He commanded that she sin no more. He was far more concerned about where the woman's heart would be at the final Judgment, than her immediate punishment.

Jesus's mission on this earth was not to condemn the world, "but that the world through Him might be saved" (John 3:17). Our mission is to introduce people to this Jesus. In following His example, we must love all people: adulterers, liars, homosexuals, thieves, etc. But a pure love cannot compromise God's standard. It cannot tolerate evil or wrongdoing. This kind of love can only hope and pray for their change of heart, and that they may some day stand before God in purity.

We need to love people. In fact God commands that we love people. There is no place in God's kingdom for religious self-righteousness. God has not called us to look down on others and condemn them for their mistakes. He desires that we walk in the humility that recognizes that we have all sinned and need grace before a holy God.

Like the corrupt tax collectors and the rich young ruler, Jesus does not condemn us. He invites us to leave our old life-style and follow Him. So let us strive for the same balanced perspective: to offer unconditional acceptance and affection for the person without tolerating immoral behavior. May we express God's unceasing love without compromising His eternal truth.

Digging Deeper:   John 4:5-42.   Romans 1.

My Prayer to my Father:

_____

_____

_____

_____

_____

I will share what I learned with: _____

# Day 29

## The Good Side of Submission

*Therefore submit to God. Resist the devil and he will flee from you.*

- James 4:7

Having grown up attending church, I have heard the last half of this verse quoted on many occasions. Most of the time, it was a well-meaning person attempting to encourage a struggling friend. In stark contrast, I have only heard the first half quoted once or twice.

We seem to have no problem attempting to be good people. We are good at going to church. We put forth an effort to be nice to people at work. We may even go so far as to read a little daily devotional book. But we seem to choke when it comes to digesting the concept of submission.

For most of us, hearing the word "submit"

135

evokes images of slavery or abusive spouses. We cringe at this thought because the master never has the slave's best interest at heart, and the abused spouse always gets hurt. In addition to the pain inflicted in both of these situations, their basic human dignity is stripped away.

But God is different. His ways are not our ways. His intentions toward us are *always* good. His love for us is unconditional. Whether we are currently battling the storms of life or enjoy smooth sailing, God always wants what is best for us.

But willful submission is still difficult, because it requires the surrendering of our own will. And we really like to be in control. We want to do what we want, and we want to do it our way. To truly submit to God means we must relinquish that control and place ourselves under His authority. In essence, we allow God to have the final say in everything we do.

Because God created us, we owe our very existence to Him. This unique Creator-creation relationship obligates us to obey His commands. Ironically, this supreme power over us is not what motivates most people to serve God.

Most people submit to God as a result of some type of inner revelation or epiphany about His love for them. His loving-kindness and goodwill toward us eliminates our doubt, fear, and hesitation to surrender everything to Him.

Our pride is the biggest thing that keeps us from coming to God. Although we rarely think about it, we tend to approach God with a remarkable amount of arrogance. We try to bribe Him or we try to make deals with Him. Amazingly, we sometimes act like He should be serving us! We get mad at Him for not doing things our way. Then we may go even farther and criticize how He runs the universe. We put ourselves on the throne and condemn God for "causing" our pain or for allowing evil to exist at all.

To counter our natural bent, God offers us grace through Jesus Christ. As a consistent principal, "God resists the proud, but gives grace to the humble" (vs. 6). We need to correct our thinking. God is not evil; He is good. He is pure, He is glorious, He is holy, and He is love.

Submission requires humility and is rewarded with grace. Since we cannot do anything good on our own, we need God's grace in order to walk in righteousness. Repentance of past sin is the first outflow of true submission. We can then walk in His grace and resist the temptations and the evil thoughts that come into our heads.

Only when we fully and consistently submit ourselves to God will we be able to effectively resist the devil. Let us then humble ourselves in the sight of the Lord, and submit to His authority (vs. 10). Only when we surrender to God can we live a life that is pleasing to Him.

Digging Deeper:   Exodus 20:3.   1 Peter 5:5.   1 John 4:4.   Deuteronomy 4:32-40.

My Prayer to my Father:

_____

_____

_____

_____

_____

I will share what I learned with: _____

# Day 30

## How to be Super Religious

*Pure and undefiled religion before God and the Father is this: to visit orphans and widows in their trouble, and to keep oneself unspotted from the world.*

- James 1:27

What does it mean to be religious? For many, it means getting dressed up and going to church, singing a few songs, and sitting through a sermon. More and more people seem to think that going through such a ritual on a weekly basis is pointless or even repulsive. To others, it is an important part of their lifestyle; they comfort themselves with the thought that God is pleased with such behavior. But is this real religion?

Church, in itself, can certainly be beneficial. We need to come together to study the Bible, worship God as a group, and encourage and pray for each other. The benefits of fellowship and unity are innumerable. We are not to avoid gathering like this (Hebrews 10:25), but simply going to church does not make you religious from God's perspective.

Going to church, like any good thing, can be abused or perverted. The motives of our heart make all the difference. If we go to church for the wrong reasons, it will do us no heavenly good. We must fight our tendency to become comfortable in our rituals and complacent in our traditions. Church activities can be good, but they do not make us good.

Some of the pomp and rituals practiced in church today are no more acceptable before God than that of the Pharisees of Jesus' day. He rebuked them for substituting the desires of God for the vain and empty traditions of men. Their religious activity did nothing to draw them closer to God, but rather, they actually stood on their religious façade in order to reject God's Messiah.

God's interests are far more intimate than outward displays of spirituality. On a personal level, if our involvement in church programs and our study of the Bible are disconnected from our relationship with God, they can lead to a great deal of pride.

What God desires, and what He considers to be true religion, is a combination of both *love* and *purity*. We are to possess outward acts of charity to those in need, especially to those without family. We are also to maintain an inward purity toward God.

Loving others must include meeting their needs. This often-unseen care for the hurting is what pleases the Almighty. God wants us to have a heart of compassion where His love can flow through us to touch the hearts of others. We are also called to love others enough to point them to Jesus and disciple them. Love involves both physical and spiritual care.

Personal purity is a gift from God that is given by grace when we place our faith in Jesus. His blood washes away our sin and empowers us to live in righteousness. "Therefore submit to God. Resist the devil and he will flee from you. Draw near to God and He will draw near to you. Cleanse your hands, you sinners; and purify your hearts, you double-minded" (James 4:7-8).

To be involved in real religion we must practice real benevolence. To be truly religious, we must put on the righteousness that comes only through faith in Jesus Christ. Both of these flow from the intimacy that God desires us to have with Him. This is the pure and undefiled religion that we are supposed to practice.

So let us seek God with all our heart. Let us abide in Jesus and walk with Him in faith throughout each day. As a child of God, let us be a brother, a sister, a son, or a mother to those that are lonely and hurting. Remember, God loves it when we love those He loves!

Digging Deeper: Matthew 25:31-46. John 4:23 & 13:35. 1 John 3:17-18 & 4:20-21.

My Prayer to my Father:

_____

_____

_____

_____

_____

I will share what I learned with: _____

# Day 31

## Speak Good

*Let no corrupt word proceed out of your mouth, but what is good for necessary edification, that it may impart grace to the hearers.*

- Ephesians 4:29

When writing to the church in Ephesus, Paul gives some very practical instructions for day-to-day living. Admonitions like this one can apply just as easily to us as it did to them.

When we lived like most other people in the world, our speech was twisted and often hurtful. Perhaps our conversation was geared toward putting other people down or puffing ourselves up.

But when we were redeemed by Christ's blood we put off our old man with his deeds, and have put on a new man, renewed in knowledge (Colossians 3:9-10). Now, in humility, we are to encourage others in their faith toward God.

We are to guard our speech carefully, saying

only those things that are good. "Good" will not always be easy to communicate or hear, but it will always be done to build up the other person. Such speech will minister God's grace to the hearer because it is spoken in love.

Why take such care in the things we say to one another? First, as children of God, we desire to live a life that is pleasing to Him. Secondly, how much we love others is a reflection of how much we love God!

How then do we make the necessary adjustments? Jesus said that out of the abundance of the heart, the mouth speaks (Matthew 12:33-37). We must, therefore, begin internally. To communicate His goodness to those around us, we must first be convinced of His goodness. We must allow God to purify our hearts and fill us with a Godly love for others. As we draw closer to Jesus, our speech will begin to shift from vile and vain to good and gracious.

Corrupt communication can include things like slander, deceit, and gossip. It flows out of our insecurity, envy, and pride; and it leaves a trail of pain, distrust, and broken relationships. Even if we look good on the outside, the things coming out of our mouths can defiled us before God (Matthew 15:7-20).

Paul is instructing us to edify others. A large building or structure is sometimes called an edifice. To edify is to "build up" someone with our speech. It also means to confirm and embolden, to instruct morally, to benefit spiritually, and to uplift. We edify people when we encourage them in, and point them toward, a closer walk with God.

Allow me to clarify a couple of other words that are to define our conversations. The word "exhort" is similar to edify. It means to call near, invite, caution, admonish urgently, and comfort.

The word "bless" comes from the same root word as "eulogy". It means to speak well of someone. When people get up to speak at a funeral, they eulogize the deceased by talking about all the good things they did, the admirable aspects of their character, and the fond memories they hold dear.

We can also bless someone who is still alive by simply speaking well of them. This is most effective, however, when we speak well of them *to them*. Like Jacob with his kids, a blessing can also be inspired by the Holy Spirit to tell of a future good that God intends to bring to pass.

Let us be diligent to guard both our heart and tongue. Let us love the people around us enough to not only *want* them to have a deep and intimate relationship with Jesus, but be willing to *speak* God's grace into their lives.

Digging Deeper:　　Luke 6:28.　Hebrews 10:23-25.
2 Peter 1:12-15.　James 3:1-12.


My Prayer to my Father:

_____

_____

_____

_____

_____


I will share what I learned with: _____

# Day 32

## United in Christ

*For you are still carnal. For where there are envy, strife, and divisions among you, are you not carnal and behaving like mere men? For when one says, "I am of Paul," and another, "I am of Apollos," are you not carnal? Who then is Paul, and who is Apollos, but ministers through whom you believed, as the Lord gave to each one? I planted, Apollos watered, but God gave the increase. So then neither he who plants is anything, nor he who waters, but God who gives the increase.*

- 1 Corinthians 3:3-7

Paul was addressing the Christians in Corinth, but he was not flattering them or giving them "warm fuzzies" at the time. A trend had begun to take place that was not in tune with the Spirit of God.

Being distinctly different from the world was not

147

enough for them. These early believers were moved by their carnal natures to search for a niche that would make them different or "better" than their brothers and sisters in Christ. They began to rally around Christian leaders, supposing one to be more highly respected than the others.

Paul refers to them as "carnal". In doing so, he was not calling them names or putting them down, but merely pointing out a fact, which their behavior had made obvious. They were being fleshly and worldly, not spiritual.

Instead of unifying around the power and glory of God, they began to exalt individuals – and by joining themselves to such men, they were attempting to exalt themselves. Such polarization and pride gave birth to contentions and divisions.

Sadly, they had been distracted from what was important. Lulled away from recognizing God as the sole supplier of spiritual blessings, they had begun to accredit such things to His servants. Paul reminds them that people are merely servants and workers, and that it is God who controls the outcome and the fruit.

Our focus and faith must remain on Jesus. We need to be reminded of this basic point as much as the Christians in Corinth. Perhaps you have heard someone proudly say that they follow Martin Luther, John Calvin, or some other famous teacher. Sometimes we align ourselves with a particular denomination because we grew up in it or think it is the most Biblical. We take pride in our church or pastor as if they are better than another. We forget that it is God who gives the spiritual increase. When asked what religion we belong to, do we proudly say, "I am a Baptist (or Assembly of God, or Methodist)," or do we say, "I am a Christian, I follow Jesus Christ?'

We must recognize that too strong of an allegiance to a man or denomination will soon lead to divisions and strife among Christians, as well as confusion and skepticism among non-believers. The deeper danger here is that if this carnality is allowed to continue, it will subtly begin to shift our faith away from what Jesus has done for us. Too much of a loyalty to a church can morph into it becoming our identity. It can effectively become the focus of our faith without us even noticing.

We should always strive to know God better. We need to study God's Word and know what we believe, but we cannot allow our defense of the faith to degrade into a defense of our church or tradition.

We must give God His place of honor. We must give God the credit for our purity and right-standing before Him, and for the spiritual growth in our lives.

God desires true unity among those who follow Him, and Jesus prayed earnestly for it. This is not a shallow unity for the sake of unity. This is a strong bond between all those who believe in and follow

Jesus. We are unified in Christ.

In everything, our ultimate allegiance and loyalty must remain with God alone. In true spirituality, we are to resist envy, pride, and unnecessary divisions. In Christ-like love, we are to offer grace, charity, and forgiveness. Only in Jesus do we have the true unity with other believers that God has called us to enjoy.

Digging Deeper:    Luke 9:49-50.   John 17:9-26.
1 Corinthians 11:13-16.   Acts 4:32.

My Prayer to my Father:

_____

_____

_____

_____

_____

I will share what I learned with: _____

# Day 33

## Ultimate Trust

*Though He slay me, yet will I trust Him.*

- Job 13:15a

What would cause a man to trust in God to this extent? Why would he be willing to place his life in the hands of someone who might take it? If being "religious" is all about self-preservation, getting to heaven, and being blessed, what did Job stand to gain by such a commitment?

It was established early in the book that Job was a righteous man. In fact, God Himself considered Job blameless and upright. His walk with God was honest and sincere even before the tragedies occurred. God had caused Job to prosper at the beginning, but Job's dedication and loyalty to God was not based on the children and wealth he was given.

Job believed that serving God was the right thing to do regardless of what happened to him. He was thoroughly convinced that God was worth it. He was committed to walking before God in purity, not because of what he would get out of it, but simply because of who God was.

There are three facts about God that inspire this kind of faith. Understanding them is fundamental to a deep, meaningful walk with God. Without a strong assurance of these basic facts, it would be easy to distrust God and turn our backs on Him.

First of all, He is our *Creator*, and He must be honored as such. "In the beginning God created the heavens and the earth" (Gen. 1:1). God formed us and gave us life. As the originator of all things, He has the power and the right to do as He wishes.

He is the Creator and we are His creation. We owe Him our very existence. Every breath we breathe is a gift from God.

Secondly, we must acknowledge that God is *Sovereign*. Even more than a king, He has authority over that which He has created. His complete control over every single thing is not without intent. There is a purpose to His ways.

When we call Him Lord, we must remember that just as the heavens are higher than the earth, His ways are higher than our ways and His thoughts are higher than our thoughts (Isaiah 55:9). We must trust that, in His wisdom, He will bring about His ultimate good, especially when we do not understand!

Thirdly, we must know that God is indeed *Good*. When disaster strikes, we have two choices. We can either trust in Him, or turn on Him.

Goodness and love are the character traits of God that are most often called into question. The single biggest lie the Adversary whispers in our ears is, "If God really loved you He would not have allowed such a bad thing to happen to you."

If we do not have full confidence in His compassion and love, we tend to blame Him instead of running to Him for help. The more we see how much God really cares for us, the easier it is to remain loyal and obey.

It is critical therefore that we strive to know Him for who He is. We cannot be content with a few facts about God filtered through other people's opinions. This will not sustain us in the tough times. We must fall at His feet, and we must worship Him in spirit, and we must worship Him in truth.

Let us then taste and see that the Lord is good. Let us diligently study His wonders and His ways. May we comprehend the infinite love of God, which was fully demonstrated by Jesus as He willingly suffered and died to wash away our sins and reconcile us to the Father. May we bow before His throne and present ourselves as living sacrifices, determined to love Him in the easy times and the hard times. Let us trust Him through the prosperous days as well as the tragedies. Let us trust Him with our very life. Although it is but a vapor, it should be lived for His glory.

Digging Deeper:    Matthew 16:24-26.   Luke 22:42. Proverbs 3:5-12.

My Prayer to my Father:

_____

_____

_____

_____

_____

I will share what I learned with: _____

# Day 34

## Patient to Perfection

*My brethren, count it all joy when you fall into various trials, knowing that the testing of your faith produces patience. But let patience have its perfect work, that you may be perfect and complete, lacking nothing.*

- James 1:2-4

When we looked at this passage in James on Day 25, we focused on the joy. Now let us focus on the patience. It is important to understand that the word "patience" meant something slightly different to James than it does to most of us now. Although the Greek word used here comes from a root word meaning "to bear trials", this word actually refers to a *cheerful* endurance or a *hopeful* waiting.

James was not alone in his sentiment toward patience. Paul also echoes the same theme: that

155

patience is indeed a good thing. His parallel statement can be found in Romans 5:3-5. In explaining the Christian's condition before God, Paul states that we have been justified by faith and have peace with God through Jesus Christ. He then goes on to say that we also glory in tribulations, knowing that tribulation will result in patience. Through patience we learn experience, and by experience we cultivate our hope.

Patience is not something that is to be dreaded, or a lesson to be avoided. Patience is part of the process that perfects our hope in God. So precious is this hope that we should welcome with joy anything that would lead to its growth and maturity - even suffering, persecution, and waiting.

Unfortunately, we spend so much of our time and energy pursuing pleasure and avoiding discomfort, that when God allows us to go through hard times in order to make us better, we resent Him instead of thanking Him.

So how do we get this good kind of patience? James says that the testing of our faith will produce it. Paul states that it will come about as a result of tribulations. Perhaps this is why we dislike it so much.

In order to appreciate patience, and the hard times that can help form it, we must truly understand the heart of God, His wisdom, and what He wants to do in us. We need to be able to look forward to the fruit or result of this cheerful waiting. According to Paul, it brought about experience and hope in God. But in the mind of James, the purpose of patience is our perfection in Christ. He said that once patience has done its work, we would be "perfect and complete, lacking nothing." This means that we will be mature and will not "fail, be destitute, or lack" anything God wants to give us. King David had some of this divine insight when he wrote in Psalm 23, "The Lord is my shepherd, I shall not want."

When you boil it down to the basics, patience is a practical expression of our faith in God. Do we really trust that He is good? Do we really trust that He is in control? Do we really trust that His timing is perfect?

God loves us and wants what is truly best for us. He wants to bless us, but not necessarily with money or things. In the end, God wants to bless us with faith, hope, and intimacy with Him.

We must surrender our life and place it completely in God's hands. When we face temptations or trials, or suffer persecution, let us wait patiently on the Lord. Let us endure with joy whatever comes our way, knowing that He will meet our needs and bring us to maturity in our faith. Let us cheerfully endure every difficulty, not with bitterness or frustration, but with the hope that God will work all things out for His good. When we do this, we will shine for His glory like a lighthouse in a storm!

Digging Deeper:    Acts 14:21-22.   Romans 8:35-39.
Hebrews 12:1-2.  1 Peter 4:19.  2 Timothy 4:1-8.
John 16:33.

My Prayer to my Father:

_____

_____

_____

_____

_____

I will share what I learned with: _____

# Day 35

## Forgiveness is Love

*And whenever you stand praying, if you have anything against anyone, forgive him, that your Father in heaven may also forgive you your trespasses. But if you do not forgive, neither will your Father in heaven forgive your trespasses.*

- Mark 11:25-26

The statement that Jesus made to his followers regarding forgiveness is simple: we must forgive others for the wrongs that they have done to us if we expect God to forgive us for the wrongs that we have done to Him.

The forgiveness that God offers us stems from His mercy and love. It is this love and mercy that God desires, and even requires us to have towards others. The principles that relate to love in 1 John 4:7-8, relate to forgiveness in this verse. Those who love God show it in the way they love other people. In the same way, those who have been forgiven by God, eagerly forgive other people.

Because of the way it is written, this verse may seem to imply that, as we forgive others, God will forgive us. The true order of events, though, is again modeled after love; we love God because He first loved us. We do not forgive in order to be forgiven, but as a result of being forgiven.

This is illustrated for us in Matthew 18:21-35. Jesus told a parable about a servant who owed a large amount of money to the king. Since the servant could not pay, he begged the king for mercy and time. Having compassion on the man, the king decided to forgive him of the entire debt. After the servant had been released of his huge debt, he encountered a fellow servant who owed him a much smaller amount of money. When his fellow servant pleaded for more time, he refused and had him thrown in jail. When the king found out what the first servant had done he was furious, and had him imprisoned. When this man refused to forgive his fellow servant, he exposed his ingratitude, arrogance, and unwillingness to reflect the king's character. In truth, our sin against God is always incomparably more severe than someone else's sin against us.

Jesus also explained to his disciples that forgiveness must be sincere and from the heart, and that it must be unlimited. This can only be done in the power of God and by understanding the magnitude of God's mercy toward us.

If we will not completely release, set free, and hold blameless those who have wronged us, then we truly do not understand the incredible magnitude of what God has done for us.

God does not forgive us just so we can go to heaven when we die. What He really wants is for us to humbly walk with Him in righteousness right now. To try to receive God's forgiveness, without offering forgiveness to those that hurt us, is to miss the whole point of what God is trying to do *in* us.

God wants us to be like Him. Forgiving us is an essential part of the process. He loves us so we can love others. He loves us enough to forgive us so that we can love others enough to forgive them.

To accept God's love and forgiveness for our selves, and yet refuse to love and forgive others is hypocritical. To be a part of the kingdom of God is to be forgiving. Someone else's choice to hurt us does not negate our obligation to love them. We cannot truly love a person that we refuse to forgive.

God wants us to value relationships and pursue reconciliation. He created us in His image and He wants us to recognize and value that image in others.

This concept of reconciliation is so prevalent that the reverse of forgiving is also true. If we know of anyone we have offended or hurt, we should even put our worship of God on pause in order to go and try to make things right with them (Matthew 5:23-24). Why is this so important? Because obeying God's command and reflecting His character is the highest form of worship, and the thing that pleases our Father the most.

Unfortunately, we often try to find excuses for not forgiving. Even Peter questioned Jesus about the limits of such extravagant love. He may have thought that forgiving someone seven times was generous enough, but Jesus pushed the number of offenses sky high (Matthew 18:21-22). Some Bible versions say we should forgive 77 times a day, some say 70x7, which would be 490. Regardless, Jesus made it abundantly clear that if you are keeping count, you are not truly forgiving them.

This can be one of the biggest hurdles a Christian has to overcome. But if we can die to ourselves and lay down our rights, few things will bring us more freedom and joy.

Therefore, let us follow Jesus's example. He forgave the people that killed Him *while* they were killing Him (Luke 23:34). We know it is possible for us mere mortals to do the same because a regular guy named Stephen did what Jesus did when they were stoning him to death (Acts 7:59-60).

God is not putting some huge, intolerable burden on us by saying that we have to forgive people. He is giving us the *opportunity* to express divine love. That is a privilege we enjoy as a child of God.

Therefore, let us forgive lavishly.

Digging Deeper:  Romans 5:6-8.  Matthew 5:43-48. 2 Corinthians 5:14-21.

My Prayer to my Father:

_____

_____

_____

_____

_____

I will share what I learned with: _____

# Day 36

## A Glimpse of God's Glory

*To you it was shown, that you might know that the LORD Himself is God; there is none other besides Him.*

- Deuteronomy 4:35

Many Christians struggle with the Old Testament. They drown in a sea of genealogy or get mired in long lists of long-ago kings. Many give up and just stick to the simple stories of Jesus and the apostles, or the wonder and intrigue of the Book of Revelation.

Unfortunately, if they do this, they will miss out on a great deal of what God has revealed about Himself. For a full and balanced picture of God, we must see the wonder of the New Testament through the light of the Old. Like walking into a theater two-thirds of the way through a movie, you might see the hero save the day, but you would miss a lot of the valuable background information that would give the ending its full impact and meaning.

In this part of Deuteronomy, Moses is reviewing the major plot points through which God has brought the Israelites. This is his last big speech to the people, and in it he recounts their history with God. He brings up their past in order to encourage them to be faithful in the future as they move into the land that God would be giving them (vs. 9).

Moses reminds them of how God delivered them as a whole nation from slavery in Egypt. God had used signs and wonders to bring them out as His people by "a mighty hand and an outstretched arm, and by great terrors" (vs. 34). They even heard the voice of God speaking out of the fire on Mount Sinai, and lived (vs. 33).

In all these things, God was revealing His glory to the children of Israel. Through all these events, God was setting them apart to know Him and represent Him like no other people. Time and time again, He had shown them His supernatural powers, displayed His mercy, and provided for their needs.

By watching God work and observing His nature, their understanding of God grew. They began to know Him on a more intimate basis (vs. 10). He did this in order to make them His own. He did this so that they would know that He is the one, true, and living God, and that they are His people and His inheritance (vs. 20).

How observant are we of God's works today? Do we give God credit and thanks for the occasional miracle in our lives? How about the daily provisions that we receive?

For thousands of years, God has revealed His divine nature and His will to individual prophets. It formed a continually growing story of an unchanging, eternal God. The more we read God's history with the people He created, the clearer we see the bigger picture. More importantly, we begin to see our world from His perspective.

Then God did something even more amazing! God revealed His glory, His limitless love, and His salvation through Jesus, His Son! (Hebrews 1:1-2)

Jesus was the Anointed One that God's people had looked for and longed for. In Him was the fullness of the Godhead in bodily form (Colossians 2:9-10). The Holy One of Israel redeemed the world back to Himself and freed us from our rebellion through the blood Jesus shed while dying on a cross.

While Jesus is the climax of the story, where does that leave us now? Do we have a hunger and desire to know God better every day? Do we actively and diligently search the Bible for revelations of His character, His grace, His holiness, and His will for our lives?

May we follow in the footsteps of the ancient followers of God. May we forsake all other gods and false ways. May we cling to the one true God with all our might and love Him with all our heart. May we marvel at the wondrous things that He has done throughout all history. May we be humbled in His presence and obedient in all that He asks of us.

Let us be faithful to our Creator. Let us acknowledge Him in all our ways, and let us praise Him and exalt Him for all that He is!

Digging Deeper:  Romans 15:4.  Hebrews 11:1-12:2.  Luke 24:25-27.

My Prayer to my Father:

_____

_____

_____

_____

_____

I will share what I learned with: _____

# Day 37

## Right and Wrong Rituals

*Though you offer Me burnt offerings and your grain offerings, I will not accept them, nor will I regard your fattened peace offerings. Take away from Me the noise of your songs, for I will not hear the melody of your stringed instruments. But let justice run down like water, and righteousness like a mighty stream.*

- Amos 5:22-24

The Bible says that God is love (1 John 4:8). Everything He says reflects His love. Everything He does flows from His character. This passage, like so many other verses, reveals the heart of our Creator.

For many centuries, God required His people to make certain sacrifices, keep certain feasts, and do certain rituals. Most of these were introduced to be a continual reminder of something amazing that God had done. Some were simply a call to worship.

Modern-day examples would include baptism and communion. Baptism is a public representation of our commitment to Jesus Christ. It symbolizes the act of dying to ourselves and being raised to new life in Christ. Communion is also a representation of our commitment to Christ as we symbolically partake of His body and blood. It is to be a continual reminder of how His body was broken for our healing and how His blood was shed for our forgiveness.

These ceremonies are a beautiful and valuable part of a Christian's life. They are great for their intended purposes, but like the offerings and songs mentioned in this passage, they can be reduced to mere rituals and become vain.

God is unimpressed with religious activity that is not founded on a sincere faith in Jesus, His Son. Our adherence to rituals does not make us righteous or good in the eyes of God. Going to Bible studies and praying before meals may fool others, but we cannot hide our hearts from Him. God is not glorified in our worship on Sunday if we are not standing up for what is right on Monday. Any sinner can perform a ritual, but God requires purity.

Judgment and righteousness flow from the heart of God. They are natural reflections of His love, and elements of His character. They are ingrained in the command to love God with our whole heart, and to love our neighbor as ourselves.

How then do we execute judgment? By upholding the law of God and making a distinction between right and wrong. The rich and powerful are not allowed to get away with sinning against God, and the sins of the poor are not ignored because we are compassionate toward their needs. There should be no partiality or favoritism in judgment. Everyone is held to the same standards, and the law is applied to everyone equally.

Being a just person and doing justice is what causes us to shine. This public display of standing up for what is right in God's eyes is a light to everyone who sees it. Proverbs 4:18 says, "But the path of the just is like the shining sun, that shines ever brighter unto the perfect day." Just like love, this is a trait that will grow inside of us for the rest of our lives.

Some of our church rituals are handed down in the form of traditions. Many of these started off with a good idea or motive, but have become so ingrained in our "American Christianity" that we forget what is Biblical and what is not. Sometimes we seem to have more faith in our traditions than we have faith in God.

If we are going to uphold traditions, we need to understand their meanings and keep them in proper perspective. If we are going to benefit from them, we need to make them personal. If we are going to keep our hearts right before God, we must abhor (passionately hate) what is evil and cling to (grab ahold of and do not let go) what is good (Romans 12:9).

Christianity is a relationship religion. The rituals are there to help us understand the relationship God is calling us into. If a ritual or tradition is ever done apart from genuine intimacy with the Father through Jesus, then it becomes a large pile of dung in God's eyes (Philippians 3:8). If we ever think that our religious traditions and rituals make us a good person or make us right in God's eyes then they have become an idol in our heart and have replaced Jesus and what He did on the cross.

Fortunately, if we have gotten distracted and self-reliant, it is never too late to turn back. Right now is always a good time to submit to God's truth and draw near to Him.

Let us place the highest priority on the things that God holds most dear. May we truly submit to God's will, and fully commit to His ways. Let us courageously stand for what is just and walk in His righteousness. When we do this, God will smile on our sacrifices, be honored by our obedience, and take pleasure in our songs!

Digging Deeper:   Micah 6:6-8.   John 6:28-29.
Galatians 3.   Isaiah 64:6.   Romans 10:1-4.


My Prayer to my Father:

_____

_____

_____

_____

_____


I will share what I learned with: _____

# Day 38

## Judas or John?

*When Jesus had said these things, He was troubled in spirit, and testified and said, "Most assuredly, I say to you, one of you will betray Me." Then the disciples looked at one another, perplexed about whom He spoke. Now there was leaning on Jesus' bosom one of His disciples, whom Jesus loved. Simon Peter therefore motioned to him to ask who it was of whom He spoke. Then, leaning back on Jesus' breast, he said to Him, "Lord, who is it?" Jesus answered, "It is he to whom I shall give a piece of bread when I have dipped it." And having dipped the bread, He gave it to Judas Iscariot, the son of Simon.*

- John 13:21-26

There were at least twelve men at the table with

Jesus that evening, but the Bible only mentions a few of them by name. One of those men was Judas Iscariot.

This man would soon betray Jesus to His face. Although Jesus could see his heart, none of the other men knew what he was planning to do. To the other disciples, everyone looked normal. To the other eleven, Judas was just like them.

He looked like a follower of Jesus. Perhaps at that moment he even acted and talked as though nothing was wrong. Yet there he was, sitting and eating before his Lord with a heart of evil and thoughts of betrayal.

Another person sitting there is described as the one "whom Jesus loved". Although he is not named, most scholars believe that this was actually John, the author, referring to himself.

In stark contrast to Judas, John is pictured leaning up against Jesus' chest. It seems clear that not only does Jesus love him, but John also loves Jesus.

It is a picture of contentment and perfect peace. This was not an assault on their masculinity, this was genuine, close friendship. Jesus had done more than pull him out of a fire or up from a pit, He had given him life itself.

Imagine for a moment, a father holding his young son in his arms. The child, feeling protected and loved, gently rests his head on his father's shoulder. He is not concerned with what others might be thinking of him. He is not worried about what might happen tomorrow. He is just enjoying the peace of the moment. That was John with Jesus.

John was adamant and unashamed about his love for Jesus. At that moment, John may have been more obedient than any other disciple with regard to the commandment to love God with all your heart, mind, and soul. He knew where he was; and more importantly, he knew Who he was with. John seemed to exemplify a mature love by balancing emotional intimacy and conscious obedience.

Let us not be like Judas. If the Messiah is not doing what we think He should, we should not try to force Him. If life is not playing out like we want or we do not understand where God is taking us, that is the time to trust and surrender. If we have bitterness, unforgiveness, or betrayal in our hearts, it must be repented of and given to God.

Unlike Judas, John is an excellent role model. Whether we are sitting before Jesus and partaking of His covenant meal, or dealing with the simple, tedious tasks of everyday life, let us learn to submerse ourselves in the peace and love that can only come as we rest on Jesus.

As I am standing at the sink, brushing my teeth and praying about how to end this chapter, the Holy Spirit gently nudges me to crawl up onto Jesus's knee like a child and put my head on His shoulder.

I do not want to just tell you to rest in His love, I want to do it myself, too. As I put my arm around Him and He puts His arm around me, I cannot wipe the smile off my face.

So come and join me. Hop up on His other knee. There is always room.

Digging Deeper:    John 2:23-25 & 15:1-17.
Matthew 11:28-30.

My Prayer to my Father:

_____

_____

_____

_____

_____

I will share what I learned with: _____

# Day 39

## Edify and Multiply

*Then the churches throughout all Judea, Galilee, and Samaria, had peace and were edified. And walking in the fear of the Lord and in the comfort of the Holy Spirit, they were multiplied.*

- Acts 9:31

We are told in Acts 8:1 that a great persecution arose against the church, scattering them throughout the regions of Judea and Samaria. This passage marks a slow-down in such attacks and conveys a growing acceptance of Christians by society.

It also gives us a glimpse at the maturity of the early church, and hints at God's overall plan for His people. It brings to light two different but vital aspects of early church life: its *spiritual growth* and its *physical growth*.

The first part of this verse speaks of them being edified, which means they were being built up and encouraged in the Lord. As persecution began to trail off, the Christian church began to settle in, carving its own little niche in society. No longer in hiding, they could begin to meet publicly and in larger groups. They would gather often to study, fellowship, and pray (Acts 2:42-43). Through these things, they were able to develop a mature faith in Jesus.

Love led them to build each other up rather than tear each other down. This type of edification had a preeminent role in the lives of the early believers. Why would it be any less vital for us today? Jesus said that the world would know that we are His disciples by our love for one another (John 13:35). This is to be a part of our ongoing lifestyle. Christians will not always enjoy peace with those around them, but we should *always* seek to love and build up one another in the faith.

The second part of this verse speaks about how the church grew. At first it seems an odd mix that the early Christians would be both afraid of God and comforted by God. In light of His self-revelation throughout the Bible, we find this is quite normal. Not only that, it seems essential to evangelism and the growth of God's kingdom.

We must see God as righteous, with the power and duty to punish sinners. When we catch glimpses of His holiness, we should tremble. If we belittle our sin, or justify it in our mind, or think we can get away with it, then we lack the appropriate fear of God.

We must also see Him as a God of love and mercy. With compassion and grace, He offers to forgive any person who puts their faith in Jesus.

But there can be a big disconnect for a lot of modern Christians. We all want to be comforted by the Great Comforter, but we do not always fear the Holy Creator. We long for God's Spirit to heal our pain, calm our anxiety, and ease our sorrow, but we hesitate to repent of our sin and give reverence to the all-powerful Holy One who will judge us in righteousness.

It is critical to understand that these two aspects of His nature work together seamlessly. It is the fear of God or awe of His majesty that often drives people to repentance, and it is the comfort and peace of His Spirit that lets us know we have found grace in His presence.

This is an ongoing thing, not just a one-time event. We are to *walk* in the fear of the Lord, and we are to *walk* in the comfort of the Holy Spirit.

With this fear and comfort, we step out with boldness and confidence to share truth with the lost. In compassion, we seek to deliver people from the wrath of God. With tenderness, we comfort the hurting and the lonely.

This is how we are to be a witness for Jesus. This is how we are to make disciples.

Multiplication of His Kingdom is a priority for God. It must be a priority for us too!

It is vital that we, as individuals, maintain an awe and reverence for our Maker. It is absolutely essential that we pursue a tender and obedient walk with the Holy Spirit. With that divine fear and comfort, may we share the good news of Jesus Christ whenever we have an opportunity.

Digging Deeper:   2 Samuel 6:1-10.   Luke 12:4-5. 2 Corinthians 1:3-4 & 7:1.   Acts 2:40-47 & 4:29-35 & 20:32.

My Prayer to my Father:

_____

_____

_____

_____

_____

I will share what I learned with: _____

# Day 40

## You are Complete!

*Beware lest anyone cheat you through philosophy and empty deceit, according to the tradition of men, according to the basic principles of the world, and not according to Christ. For in Him dwells all the fullness of the Godhead bodily; and you are complete in Him, who is the head of all principality and power.*

- Colossians 2:8-10

Ok, let us cut to the chase with this verse: Who we *are* is irrevocably connected to who Jesus *is*! If we do not know who Jesus is, we will never know who we are designed to be in Him.

But there are big obstacles to truly knowing who Jesus is, and two of the biggest ones are our faulty logic and our empty traditions. The warning Paul gives here is clear: Do not be deceived!

It is so easy to be seduced away from the truth.

Lies swirl around us constantly. They can be ideas from others, or thoughts from within. I also believe that Satan can whisper thoughts into our minds in order to entice us away from God.

We need to be on our guard. Much of the New Testament writings are theological warnings because even that first generation of Christians got off track on a regular basis.

Philosophy and tradition are not the only things that deceive us and cheat us. The love of money can cause us to stray from the faith (1 Timothy 6:10). Profane talk and the contradictions of what is falsely called science can also cause us to stray from the faith (1 Timothy 6:20-21).

This is a war for our mind and our heart. We cannot take it lightly. God wants us to stand strong in the faith and endure till the end. In His grace, He gives us everything we need to be victorious. The weapons we have are not physical, but they are mighty in God for casting down worldly arguments and the logic that exalts itself against the knowledge of God. We are to capture every thought that crosses our mind and make it obedient to Christ and consistent with His love (2 Corinthians 10:4-6).

It does not take long to realize that it is not easy to guard our mind. We are bombarded with ungodly thoughts daily. There are many scientists that try to convince us that we are evolved accidents of mutated matter. There are relentless messages that imply we need to have the right car, the right partner, the right bank account, and the right body in order to be happy. Then there are the thoughts of shame, regret, anxiety, and depression - all telling us that we will never measure up. There are also thoughts of bitterness, vengeance, and lust that seek to control us. All of these are lies.

We need to walk in truth, but what is truth? That is the question Pilate asked Jesus, but he did not stick around for the answer (John 18:38). Jesus had told His disciples, "If you abide in My word, you are My disciples indeed. And you shall know the truth, and the truth shall make you free" (John 8:31-32).

Some time after that, Jesus explained to His disciples that He was the truth (John 14:6), and that He and the Father were one (John 10:30).

In the main passage above, Paul is explaining to the Colossians that all the fullness of the Godhead dwells in Jesus, and that Jesus is the head of all principality and power (also 1:19). Jesus is divine. Jesus is deity. Jesus is God (John 1:1). All authority in heaven and on earth has been given to Him by the Father (Matthew 28:18).

He loves us, redeems us, and adopts us into His family (Romans 8:15, Ephesians 1:5). We are complete in Jesus! If we are not complete, spiritually whole, emotionally satisfied, and content in Christ, then we have been cheated. We have been lied to. We have been snookered out of our identity and robbed of our joy.

God wants to bless us. He wants His Spirit to fill us in every way. He has shown us the path of life: in His presence is fullness of joy, at His right hand are pleasures forevermore (Psalms 16:11).

In Christ, we lack nothing. We are complete and whole. We are sons and daughters of the Most High God. That is not just a cute little title; that is the reality of our new identity. We are infinitely loved and secure. Now is the time for us to believe it and live like it!

Digging Deeper: James 1:4. Proverbs 16:25. Isaiah 26:3. 2 Timothy 3. Ephesians 3:14-19 & 4:11-16.

My Prayer to my Father:

_____

_____

_____

_____

_____

I will share what I learned with: _____

# About the Author

Michael Pearson has earned a Bachelor's Degree in Church Ministries from Southeastern University in Lakeland, Florida. He has served on multiple mission trips to other countries, and spent 18 years in Utah. During that time, he preached regularly at the Salt Lake Rescue Mission, did street ministry, and served for almost 5 years as Senior Chaplain in the Salt Lake County Jail. Michael now lives with his family in Raleigh, North Carolina.

For more content and videos, or to book Michael as a speaker, please visit us at:

# www.AdventuresInDiscipleship.com